EVERYDAY WISDOM

A MODERN GUIDE TO MASTERING COMMON SENSE

ANKUR & VANDANA MEHROTRA

ISBN
Paperback 979-8-89277-203-7
Hardcase 979-8-89699-377-3

Contents

"In understanding the common-sense of others,
we discover the extraordinary in the ordinary"
— Vandana

Part 1: The Essence of Common-Sense

1. Introduction: The Lost Art of Common-Sense

- Why is common-sense so uncommon today?
- The rise of complexity and the need for simplicity.
- Information overload, critical thinking decline, and reliance on algorithms.

2. What Is Common-Sense?

- Historical, cultural, and psychological perspectives.
- Comparison with intuition, logic, and wisdom.
- The role of experience and exposure in shaping common-sense.

3. The Pillars of Common-Sense

- Observation: Seeing reality clearly.
- Critical Thinking: Honing practical judgement.
- Awareness: Staying attuned to surroundings and emotions.

Part 2: Mastering Common-Sense in Daily Life

4. The Power of Simplicity

- Simplifying decisions for better outcomes.
- Case studies of innovation through simplicity.

5. Practical Decision-Making

- Applying common-sense to solve real-world challenges.
- Frameworks for effective, grounded decisions.

6. The Role of Emotional Intelligence in Common-Sense

- Balancing logic with empathy in interactions.
- Emotional awareness as a cornerstone of practical wisdom.

7. Common-Sense in Relationships

- Communicating effectively and resolving conflicts.
- Building trust and respect through everyday wisdom.

Part 3: Overcoming Barriers to Common-Sense

8. Breaking Through Biases

- Recognising and addressing mental blind spots.
- Tackling confirmation bias, groupthink, and cultural conditioning.

9. Dealing with Information Overload

- Filtering noise and focusing on the essential.
- Strategies for critical thinking in a data-driven world.

10. The Courage to Be Practical

- Embracing practicality in a world of trends and complexity.
- Stories of individuals who prioritised common-sense.

Part 4: Cultivating Everyday Wisdom

11. Observation: The Gateway to Wisdom

- Techniques for strengthening observation skills.
- The role of mindfulness in clear perception.

12. Critical Thinking as a Lifelong Habit

- Developing analytical skills for everyday situations.
- Avoiding overthinking and finding practical solutions.

13. Awareness and Adaptability

- Staying present and responsive to change.
- Lessons from successful individuals who embody awareness.

Part 5: Common-Sense in the Modern Era

14. The Intersection of Common-Sense and Technology

- Using common-sense to navigate the digital age.
- Balancing tech reliance with human judgement.
- AI/ML and Common-Sense

15. Common-Sense and Leadership

- How leaders use practical wisdom to inspire and guide.
- Stories of influential leaders who champion common-sense.
- Additional Leadership Stories from New-Age Startups and Unicorns

16. Everyday Wisdom for a Better Tomorrow

- Applying common-sense to drive meaningful change.
- Building a future rooted in empathy, practicality, and awareness.

Part 6: Taking Action and Building Your Wisdom

17. Rediscovering the Art of Common-Sense

- Summarising the journey and lessons learned.
- Encouraging readers to embrace common-sense as a skill.

18. Your Common-Sense Toolkit

- Practical exercises and habits for mastering common-sense.
- A 30-day action plan to integrate wisdom into daily life.

Acknowledgements

Writing *Everyday Wisdom: A Modern Guide to Mastering Common-Sense* has been an extraordinary journey, one that would not have been possible without the unwavering support, guidance, and inspiration of many incredible individuals.

First and foremost, we are deeply grateful to our family, who have been our pillars of strength and our greatest teachers.

Our parents, whose life lessons and resilience became the foundation of our understanding of common-sense, thank you for showing us the beauty of wisdom in everyday moments.

To our friends and mentors, who have always encouraged us to question norms and see the world through fresh eyes, your perspectives have enriched our life and this book.

Thank you for challenging us, inspiring us, and believing in this endeavour.

A special thanks to our readers and the community of thinkers, dreamers, and doers who value the art of simplicity in an increasingly complex world. Your curiosity and hunger for clarity have been a constant source of motivation.

To the unsung heroes in our journey—the everyday people whose actions, big or small, have demonstrated the profound power of common-sense—this book is a tribute to you.

Finally, to the higher power that guides us all, reminding us to pause, reflect, and find wisdom in the ordinary—thank you for being the silent force behind every word written here.

This book is a collective reflection of experiences, shared moments, and the timeless wisdom that lives within us all.

May it serve as a reminder to embrace the extraordinary potential of our everyday lives.

With gratitude,

Ankur & Vandana

Why this book?

Have you ever found yourself questioning widely accepted norms or navigating a situation where common-sense seemed in short supply?

The Paradox of Common-Sense?

Is common-sense subjective, shaped by personal experiences, or is it a universal truth?

Let us take you on a journey through some defining moments of our life where the idea of common-sense was both a puzzle and a paradox. These experiences taught us that common-sense, far from being universal, often thrives in shades of subjectivity.

Vandana's Encounter 1: The Time Tangle with Friends

One day, my friends and I planned a get-together. To me, being on time was simply a matter of respect—a fundamental aspect of common-sense. Yet, as the hours slipped by, I found myself growing increasingly frustrated. Some friends arrived fashionably late, dismissing the importance of punctuality.

Unable to hold back, I said, *"Why can't you understand the importance of being on time? It's just common-sense!"*

Their response floored me: *"For you, maybe, but not for us. Who decides what's common-sense anyway?"*

In that moment, I realised that what seems self-evident to one person might be entirely invisible to another.

The straightforward had morphed into a riddle.

Vandana's Encounter 2: Conflicts in the Workplace

Common-sense became a recurring theme in my professional life, particularly in navigating disagreements.

There was a moment during a project when I spotted a critical issue and raised it immediately, thinking it was obvious to act swiftly. To my surprise, my peers didn't share my urgency. Heated debates ensued, with others arguing that what I saw as common-sense might not be as clear to them.

This clash was another reminder of the subjective nature of common-sense.

What felt like second nature to me seemed overly cautious or unnecessary to others.

Vandana's Encounter 3: The Business Decision Conundrum

In the complex world of decision-making, common-sense often takes centre stage—but not always in harmony.

There was a crucial moment when I had to advocate for a particular course of action, firmly believing it was the obvious, sensible choice.

Yet, as discussions unfolded, it became clear that others didn't see it that way. To them, my "obvious" solution was anything but clear-cut.

The clash of perspectives was like trying to solve a puzzle with missing pieces.

It hit me hard—common-sense, it seemed, was a mosaic of experiences, values, and beliefs.

The Paradox of Common-Sense

These encounters in life and business revealed an uncomfortable truth: common-sense is rarely universal. Instead, it's deeply influenced by our upbringing, environment, and individual perspectives.

My journey through these paradoxes taught me that common-sense is like a skill—one that needs to be cultivated with understanding and empathy.

When we acknowledge its subjectivity, we open the door to deeper connections and more meaningful solutions.

My Learning: Bridging the Gap in Understanding

Life has a way of teaching us that the rarity of common-sense is its greatest challenge and its greatest opportunity. By embracing its subjectivity, we grow in understanding, resilience, and the ability to navigate diverse perspectives.

> *"The paradox of common-sense is that its rarity challenges us to cultivate it diligently, for in its scarcity lies the opportunity for profound growth."*
> *— Vandana*

What moments in your life have challenged your perception of common-sense?

How can you cultivate this skill to bridge gaps, foster understanding, and navigate life's complexities?

Sharing our stories when common-sense meets logic: Stories from a Marriage and Business Partnership

Building a life and a business together is like juggling 2 fiery torches while riding a unicycle. For Ankur and Vandana, the challenges often boiled down to one thing: our vastly different interpretations of *common-sense*.

I, Vandana, believe that common-sense is the instinctive ability to make quick, practical decisions. For Ankur—an IIT post graduate and a corporate top performer—common-sense is rooted in logic, data, and reasoning. While these differences made us a formidable team, they also led to some hilariously frustrating moments.

Here are 3 stories from our journey that highlight our disconnect and the lessons we learned.

The Mysterious Case of the Broken Printer

One morning, we had an urgent deadline for a client proposal. Naturally, our trusty printer decided to go on strike. I smacked the side of the machine and hit the power button a few times, confident that this *common-sense trick* would work.

"Vandana, stop!" Ankur exclaimed, horrified. "That's not how you solve a problem. We need to troubleshoot systematically."

He whipped out the printer manual, started running diagnostics, and Googled "common printer issues." Meanwhile, I borrowed a USB drive, walked to the print shop down the road, and got the job done.

When I returned with the printed proposal, Ankur was still engrossed in a YouTube video about printer maintenance.

"See? Common-sense," I said smugly.

"But you didn't fix the printer," he argued.

"And yet, the problem was solved," I replied, handing him the neatly bound documents.

Lesson Learned: Sometimes, quick fixes and practical thinking save the day, even if they don't follow a step-by-step approach.

The Great Hiring Debate

As our business grew, we needed to hire a marketing manager. Ankur created a detailed scoring matrix, complete with weighted criteria for skills, experience, and cultural fit. I, on the other hand, trusted my gut.

"Vandana, intuition isn't a hiring strategy," he said, presenting his spreadsheet like it was the Ark of the Covenant.

"Ankur, people aren't spreadsheets. Sometimes, you just *feel* that someone is the right fit," I replied.

The first candidate I liked didn't meet his criteria, but I insisted. Three months later, she turned out to be one of our best hires.

"You got lucky," Ankur muttered.

"No, I trusted my common-sense," I retorted with a grin.

Lesson Learned: Data-driven decisions are essential, but intuition has its place, especially when it comes to understanding people.

3: The Social Media Showdown

When we decided to build our online presence, I suggested we post casual, relatable content to connect with our audience. Ankur, however, wanted meticulously curated posts backed by market research.

"We need to analyse our audience demographics, peak engagement times, and trending hashtags," he said, diving into analytics.

"Or we could just post something real – my journey from struggles to success, showing our emotional side and see what happens," I countered.

To prove my point, I wrote a LinkedIn article captioned, *"To Hell with Circumstances, I create Opportunities!"* The post went viral in 2017

"That's not strategy," Ankur protested.

"No, it's common-sense. People like authenticity," I replied.

Lesson Learned: Overthinking can stifle creativity. Sometimes, simplicity and authenticity are the best strategies.

The Bigger Picture

Through these moments of misalignment, we've come to realise that our differences are our greatest strength. Ankur's logical, detail-oriented approach ensures we stay grounded and make informed decisions. My instinctive, common-sense perspective brings agility and practicality to the table.

Together, we've learned that there's no singular definition of common-sense—it's a blend of experience, perspective, and personality. The key is respecting each other's viewpoints and finding a balance between instinct and reasoning.

Takeaway: Whether in marriage or business, the real magic happens when you stop trying to be "right" and start appreciating what the other person brings to the table.

As I often remind Ankur (with a wink): "It's not about whose approach is better—it's about making it work together."

About the Authors

Ankur and Vandana – The Common-Sense Rebel and the Rational Sage

Behind every great book is a story, and behind this book are 2 very different minds—joined by love, life, and a shared passion for wisdom. Meet Vandana, the champion of common-sense and intuition, and her husband, Ankur, the analytical powerhouse who thrives on logic and reasoning. Together, they bring you *Everyday Wisdom: A Modern Guide to Mastering Common-Sense*, a harmonious blend of heart and mind (with a few friendly skirmishes along the way).

The Great "Salt" Debate

Take, for instance, the time we argued over something as mundane as salt in a dish. As Vandana sprinkled salt directly into the pot with the confidence of a master chef, Ankur raised a sceptical eyebrow.

"Did you measure that?" he asked.

"Of course not," Vandana replied. "It's common-sense—enough to taste but not too much."

"Common-sense? Or reckless improvisation?" he quipped. "You know, scientifically, one teaspoon per cup is ideal."

By the end of dinner, the salt was perfect.

"See?" Vandana teased, "My common-sense wins again."

Ankur retorted, "Or maybe your intuitiveness just got lucky."

The Business Meeting Showdown

In one of our ventures as business partners, we once faced a heated debate over a client proposal.

"This pitch doesn't feel right," Vandana said, frowning over the draft.

"Feel? What does 'feel' have to do with this?" Ankur asked, diving into a spreadsheet. "The data clearly shows this is the best approach."

"But my gut says the client won't resonate with this," Vandana insisted.

"The client doesn't care about your gut," he said. "They care about numbers."

Fast forward to the meeting—the client leaned back in their chair and said, "This proposal is good, but something feels off."

Ankur gave Vandana a side-eye.

"Fine," he whispered, "Your gut gets a point this time."

Our Parenting "Crisis"

Parenting brought its own set of hilarious battles. When our child was learning to ride a bike, Ankur suggested reading articles on the biomechanics of balance.

"Just let them get on and try!" Vandana laughed.

"But if they understand the physics, they'll fall less!" Ankur protested.

"Or we could use common-sense, and you could hold the bike steady," she said, already pushing the bike forward.

So, over the years, these light-hearted debates have become our secret sauce. Vandana's heart-driven common-sense and Ankur's brainy rationality might clash, but they also complement each other beautifully. While one dream is big, the other grounds the dream in reality. When one leaps, the other calculates the distance. It's a partnership of opposites that brings balance, depth, and a lot of laughter to both life and work.

Together, we've learned that the heart and the mind aren't adversaries—they're allies.

And in this book, we've poured our combined wisdom—her intuitive leaps and his logical steps—into guiding you toward a life enriched by both common-sense and rational thought.

As we like to say: *"She's the spark; he's the fuse. Together, we ignite ideas."*

The Turning Point

Vandana has always been a firm believer in the power of common-sense, calling it her "superpower." Throughout her professional journey, entrepreneurial ventures, and even her spiritual growth, she has leaned on this one core skill to navigate challenges and find clarity. For her, common-sense isn't just about practicality—it's about connecting the dots, simplifying the complex, and making life work in harmony.

Ankur, on the other hand, comes from a world of logic and analysis. As a top-performing IIT post graduate who thrived in his corporate career, Ankur excelled by relying on deep reasoning and structured problem-solving. When the 2 of them left their secure jobs to dive into entrepreneurship, they brought very different strengths to the table—and very different perspectives.

For years, their contrasting approaches often led to spirited debates, misunderstandings, and sometimes hilarious disagreements, especially when Vandana would say, "It's just common-sense!" To Ankur, common-sense needed reasoning and data to back it up. To Vandana, common-sense was her guide, rooted in experience and intuition.

It wasn't until a curious twist of fate that Ankur truly grasped the depth of Vandana's gift. One day, a close friend approached him with a simple request:

"My friend is working on a PhD research project on common-sense in small and medium-sized entrepreneurs. Can I connect him with you?"

Without hesitation, Ankur replied, "Well, in that case, it's not me. Vandana is the right person. She keeps saying her entire journey—professional, entrepreneurial, and even spiritual—is built on one thing: common-sense."

That conversation sparked a deep and eye-opening interview for the research project, lasting over 2 hours. As Vandana shared her insights, her clarity of thought and ability to weave together lessons from diverse areas of life left Ankur in awe. For the first time, he saw her unique skill not just as an intangible trait but as an extraordinary tool—a perspective so simple yet profound that it could illuminate paths for countless others.

Inspired by that moment of realisation, they decided to work on a book together. While Vandana brings her lived experiences and wisdom shaped by her "common-sense compass," Ankur contributes his analytical rigour and ability to break down concepts. Together, they share both perspectives, blending intuition and logic to create a narrative that resonates with everyone—whether you're seeking solutions for your business, relationships, or personal growth.

This book is not just a journey into the essence of common-sense; it's a testament to how 2 contrasting minds can come together to create something meaningful, impactful, and timeless.

Preface

What is Common-Sense?

Common-sense is the knack of seeing things as they are and doing things as they ought to be done. – Harriet Beecher Stowe

In our journey through life, there's a compass we often overlook—a tool more valuable than complex theories or technical expertise. That compass is **common-sense**, often referred to as *practical wisdom*. It's the ability to make sound, reasoned judgements in everyday situations, guiding us to act with clarity and purpose.

But what exactly is common-sense? Is it an innate gift or a skill we can cultivate? And how can it become a cornerstone of living a fulfilling, effective, and balanced life?

This book delves into the essence of common-sense, offering insights, real-life examples, and actionable tips to make it an integral part of your daily existence.

> **"Common-sense is instinct, and**
> **enough of it is genius"**
> **– Josh Billings**

Understanding Common-Sense

Common-sense is the art of applying practical knowledge and good judgement to navigate the complexities of life. It bridges the gap between knowing and doing, enabling us to adapt to different circumstances, solve problems effectively, and make decisions that serve us and those around us.

While it may seem instinctive, the truth is that common-sense is a combination of:

- **Experience:** Learning from our own actions and those of others.

- **Critical Thinking:** Analysing situations and making reasoned choices.

- **Awareness:** Observing the world with an open and discerning mind.

The good news? While some aspects of common-sense may come naturally, it's largely a skill that can be nurtured and developed with intentional effort.

The Essence of Common-Sense in Everyday Life

"Common-sense is not so common."
— Voltaire

Let's illustrate common-sense in action through scenarios that resonate universally:

1. Looking Both Ways Before Crossing the Street

- One of the first lessons taught in childhood is to look both ways before stepping onto a road. This act embodies practical wisdom—anticipating potential danger and taking preventive measures.

2. Using an Umbrella in the Rain

- When the skies open up, grabbing an umbrella is common-sense. It's a simple, intuitive response to protect yourself from discomfort and inconvenience.

3. Checking the Gas Gauge Before a Road Trip

- Before embarking on a long journey, it's wise to ensure the fuel tank is full. This foresight prevents avoidable disruptions and demonstrates proactive thinking.

4. Turning Off Lights When Leaving a Room

- A small action with a big impact—turning off lights conserves energy and reduces bills. It's an everyday example of aligning behaviour with practical outcomes.

5. Using Oven Mitts When Handling Hot Cookware

- Reaching for oven mitts before handling a hot pan is a reflex born of common-sense. It highlights how simple precautions can prevent unnecessary harm.

6. Checking the Weather Before Outdoor Plans

- Before organising a picnic or hike, it's logical to check the weather forecast. This habit ensures preparedness and prevents disappointment.

7. Bringing a Jacket in Cold Weather

- Anticipating the chill of a cold day, common-sense prompts us to carry a jacket. It's a practical response to maintain comfort and health.

8. Saving Money for Future Expenses

- Financial preparedness is a hallmark of common-sense. Setting aside savings for unforeseen events reflects a grounded understanding of life's uncertainties.

9. Being Polite and Respectful

- Treating others with kindness and consideration isn't just social etiquette—it's a reflection of emotional intelligence and practical wisdom.

10. Reading Instructions Before Assembling Furniture

- Taking the time to read assembly instructions may seem tedious, but it saves time and frustration in the long run. It's a practical way to approach tasks efficiently.

Practical Tips to Cultivate Common-Sense

1. Observe More, React Less

- Pay attention to the world around you. Awareness is the first step to practical wisdom.

2. Learn from Experience

- Reflect on past decisions—what worked, what didn't, and why. Use these lessons as a guide.

3. Ask Simple Questions

- When faced with choices, ask yourself: *Does this make sense? What's the logical next step?*

4. Seek Diverse Perspectives

- Engage with people from different walks of life. Their experiences can offer fresh insights.

5. Practice Patience

- Rash decisions often lack wisdom. Take a moment to think through your actions.

6. Stay Curious

- Cultivate a mindset of lifelong learning. The more you know, the more you grow.

Reflection and Takeaway

Common-sense is not a mystical gift reserved for a few; it's a skill we all possess and can enhance with effort. It's the bridge between knowledge and action, helping us make decisions that are practical, ethical, and impactful.

Powerful Questions for Reflection:

1. In what areas of your life could you apply more common-sense?

2. How often do you rely on intuition versus analysis in decision-making?

3. What small habits can you develop to sharpen your practical wisdom?

*"Practical wisdom is the art of making
simple choices that lead to extraordinary results."*
– Vandana

Embrace common-sense as a way of life, and watch it transform your everyday experiences into a journey of purpose and fulfilment.

The Transformative Power of Common-Sense

Mastering common-sense doesn't just lead to practical benefits— it profoundly enhances your overall satisfaction and purpose. By improving decision-making, nurturing relationships, excelling professionally, and fostering spiritual growth, common-sense becomes a cornerstone for a life well-lived.

How can you integrate common-sense into your daily actions to create a more fulfilling and meaningful life?

"Success is not about complexity; it is about clarity of thought and the courage to act with common-sense." – Vandana

Let the simplicity and wisdom of common-sense guide you toward a brighter, balanced, and more meaningful tomorrow.

Unlocking the Benefits of Common-Sense

Mastering common-sense is not merely a skill; it's a transformative tool that shapes your journey across personal, professional, and spiritual realms.

Warren Buffett's Common-sense Investment Philosophy - One of the modern exemplars of common-sense-infused critical thinking is Warren Buffett, the legendary investor. Buffett's investment philosophy revolves around a common-sense approach to understanding businesses and making decisions based on their fundamental value. By distilling complex financial matters into straightforward principles, Buffett exemplifies how common-sense serves as the bedrock for astute critical thinking.

Consider Buffett's famous quote:

Rule No. 1: Never lose money.

Rule No. 2: Never forget Rule No. 1

This seemingly simple wisdom encapsulates the essence of common-sense guiding critical decisions in the complex world of finance.

Let's explore how this profound yet simple wisdom can enhance every aspect of life.

In Personal Life: The Foundation of Everyday Fulfilment

1. Effective Decision-Making

Common-sense serves as a compass for navigating life's complexities. It equips you with practical wisdom, enabling sound decisions in everyday situations.

- *Example*: Imagine deciding between a flashy gadget and saving for an emergency. Common-sense helps prioritise long-term security over short-term pleasure.

2. Problem-Solving Skills

When faced with challenges, common-sense fosters critical analysis and practical solutions.

- *Reflection*: Think about a time you solved a pressing issue by identifying the root cause instead of reacting emotionally. That's common-sense in action.

3. Interpersonal Relationships

Healthy relationships thrive on communication, empathy, and understanding—qualities that mastering common-sense amplifies.

- *Insight*: A simple gesture, like active listening, often resolves conflicts and deepens bonds.

4. Emotional Resilience

Life's ups and downs test emotional strength. Common-sense helps navigate these fluctuations with grace and resilience.

- *Takeaway*: When you focus on solutions rather than problems, you remain composed, even in adversity.

In Professional Life: A Path to Excellence

1. Leadership Skills

Great leaders rely on common-sense to guide teams with wisdom and pragmatism.

- *Perspective*: The ability to balance data-driven decisions with human insight is what sets exceptional leaders apart.

2. Critical Thinking

In a world overflowing with information, common-sense sharpens critical thinking. It enables professionals to analyse situations, identify opportunities, and make strategic choices.

- *Actionable Tip*: Ask yourself, "What's the simplest and most effective way to achieve this goal?"

3. Adaptability

The modern workplace demands flexibility. Common-sense fosters adaptability, making you agile in shifting circumstances.

- *Case Study*: Think of professionals who thrived during unexpected changes, like the rise of remote work. Their success stemmed from practical thinking and rapid adaptation.

4. Conflict Resolution

Common-sense is invaluable in resolving workplace conflicts. It encourages diplomatic solutions that maintain harmony.

- *Scenario*: In a disagreement, understanding all perspectives and finding common ground reflects the power of practical wisdom.

In Spiritual Life: A Journey Toward Inner Peace

1. Ethical Decision-Making

At its core, common-sense aligns with ethical reasoning. It guides you in making morally sound decisions that resonate with spiritual values.

- *Reflection*: Consider the impact of your choices on yourself, others, and the environment. This awareness strengthens your spiritual path.

2. Mindfulness and Presence

Living in the present moment becomes effortless with common-sense as your anchor. It fosters mindfulness and deepens your spiritual journey.

- *Practice*: Cultivate awareness by asking, "What is the most meaningful way I can spend this moment?"

3. Compassion and Empathy

The interconnectedness of all beings becomes apparent when common-sense merges with compassion and empathy.

- *Insight*: Small acts of kindness, grounded in common-sense, ripple into profound spiritual growth.

4. Balanced Living

Harmonising personal, professional, and spiritual aspects of life requires balance—a hallmark of common-sense.

- *Takeaway*: A balanced approach to life leads to holistic well-being and a purposeful existence.

Chapter 1

Introduction:
The Lost Art of Common-Sense

*"Common-sense is genius dressed
in its working clothes."*
– Ralph Waldo Emerson

Why is common-sense, once considered the bedrock of practical decision-making, increasingly rare today? Despite the wealth of information and technological advancements, we often find ourselves over-complicating the simplest aspects of life. Have we, in our pursuit of innovation and progress, overlooked the profound wisdom of common-sense?

This chapter explores the phenomenon of its decline, the factors contributing to its obscurity, and the urgent need to rediscover and embrace this timeless skill.

Why Is Common-Sense So Uncommon Today?

Common-sense, often defined as sound judgement in everyday matters, seems paradoxically elusive in our modern world. The reasons are multi-faceted:

1. The Rise of Complexity

In an era dominated by hyper-specialisation and sophisticated technologies, simplicity often takes a backseat. We celebrate experts with niche knowledge while undervaluing the ability to distil complex ideas into practical, actionable insights.

Example:

Ratan Tata, one of India's most iconic business leaders, displayed unparalleled common-sense when spearheading the Tata Nano project. He observed that Indian families often travelled dangerously on two-wheelers and envisioned an affordable car as a solution. His focus was simple: safety, affordability, and accessibility. While the project faced challenges, the idea originated from an astute observation of everyday life and a common-sense approach to solving a real problem.

2. Information Overload

We live in an age of excess information. While knowledge is at our fingertips, discernment—the ability to separate the wheat from the chaff—has diminished. Bombarded by data, we often lose sight of practical and straightforward solutions.

Example:

Steve Jobs, co-founder of Apple, was known for his obsession with simplicity. The iPhone was revolutionary not just because of its technology but because of how seamlessly it integrated into everyday life. Jobs frequently said, *"Simple can be harder than complex. You have to work hard to get your thinking clean to make it simple."* His common-sense approach to technology made Apple products accessible, intuitive, and universally loved.

3. Decline in Critical Thinking

Critical thinking, a cornerstone of common-sense, is in decline. The prevalence of echo chambers, social media algorithms, and groupthink has led to a collective erosion of individual judgement.

Example:

Closer to home, Narayana Murthy, co-founder of Infosys, built one of India's most successful IT companies by adhering to simple yet powerful principles: integrity, customer focus, and teamwork. While many companies chased short-term profits, Murthy's practical wisdom ensured sustainable growth and long-term impact. His ability to think critically and act on common-sense principles set Infosys apart in a competitive industry.

The Need for Simplicity in a Complex World

The world today is more connected yet more complicated than ever. Rediscovering the power of simplicity is not just a choice—it's a necessity.

Practical Tip:

When faced with a challenge, ask yourself, *"What's the simplest way to address this issue without compromising quality?"* Simplifying doesn't mean cutting corners; it means removing unnecessary complexity to focus on what truly matters.

The Role of Algorithms and the Decline of Intuition

Reliance on algorithms and artificial intelligence is growing. While these tools have their place, an over-dependence on them can erode our ability to make sound judgements.

Example:

Captain Chesley "Sully" Sullenberger, the pilot who safely landed a US Airways plane on the Hudson River, relied on years of experience and common-sense when the engines failed mid-flight. While algorithms and protocols dictated other options, Sully's practical wisdom saved 155 lives. This incident reminds us that even in a world dominated by technology, human judgement and common-sense are irreplaceable.

Restoring Common-Sense: Stories That Inspire

1. Dhirubhai Ambani:

Dhirubhai, the founder of Reliance Industries, built his empire by observing market trends and leveraging simple yet effective strategies. His ability to understand the pulse of the common man—whether it was affordable polyester or accessible financial services—demonstrated an exceptional grasp of common-sense in business.

2. Oprah Winfrey:

Oprah's journey from poverty to becoming a media mogul was guided by her ability to connect with people on a deeply human level. Her common-sense approach to storytelling—asking what her audience truly needed—created a brand that resonated worldwide.

Practical Tips for Cultivating Common-Sense

1. Slow Down:

Pause before making decisions. Ask yourself: *Is this the simplest, most logical course of action?*

2. Observe the Basics:

Like Ratan Tata, pay attention to everyday challenges around you. Often, the best ideas are hidden in plain sight.

3. Challenge Complexity:

When faced with overwhelming data, simplify by asking: *What is the core issue? What solution would make the biggest impact?*

4. Trust Your Experience:

Practical wisdom is built over time. Reflect on past experiences and use them as a guide.

Conclusion

Common-sense is not just a relic of the past; it's a skill for the future. In a world increasingly drawn to complexity, the ability to think simply and act wisely is more valuable than ever.

"Common-sense is not about knowing everything; it's about knowing what truly matters and acting on it." – Ankur

Reflection Questions

1. In what areas of your life do you tend to overcomplicate decisions?

2. How often do you prioritise simplicity over complexity in your personal and professional life?

3. Can you think of a recent situation where common-sense would have led to a better outcome?

Plan of Action

1. Practice Observation:

Spend 10 minutes daily observing your surroundings. Look for simple patterns or overlooked details.

2. Simplify Decisions:

For one week, consciously eliminate unnecessary steps in daily tasks. Reflect on the outcomes.

3. Cultivate Awareness:

Limit distractions, especially digital ones, for at least an hour each day. Use this time to think critically about a challenge you're facing.

By embracing simplicity, critical thinking, and awareness, we can reclaim the lost art of common-sense and navigate life's complexities with grace and wisdom.

Chapter 2

What is Common-Sense?

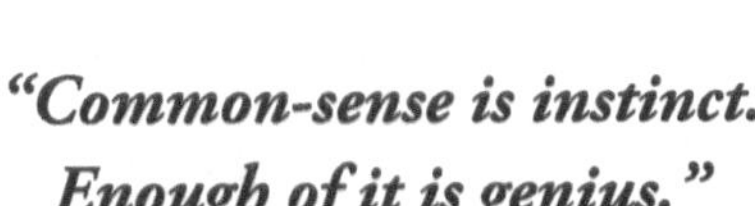

"Common-sense is instinct.
Enough of it is genius."
– George Bernard Shaw

Common-sense is often hailed as the unsung hero of decision-making, yet its definition remains elusive. Is it an innate ability, a learned skill, or a blend of both? This chapter unravels the concept of common-sense through historical, cultural, and psychological lenses, explores how it differs from intuition, logic, and wisdom, and examines the role of experience in shaping it.

A Historical Perspective: The Evolution of Common-Sense

The roots of common-sense trace back to ancient civilisations.

1. Greek Origins:

The term "common-sense" originates from the Latin *sensus communis*, a concept Aristotle described as the collective ability to perceive and interpret sensory experiences. For Aristotle, common-sense was a critical function of the human mind, allowing individuals to make coherent judgements.

2. The Enlightenment Era:

During the 18th century, Scottish philosopher Thomas Reid argued that common-sense was the foundation of all human knowledge. He believed that practical judgement, rooted in shared human experience, was more reliable than abstract theories.

3. Modern Times:

In today's world, common-sense is often seen as the bridge between intellectual reasoning and everyday decision-making. While its essence has remained constant, its application has evolved with societal changes.

Example:

Mahatma Gandhi's philosophy of nonviolence is a shining example of common-sense in action. He observed that violence only perpetuated suffering and sought a solution rooted in simplicity and practicality. His approach united millions and proved that profound changes could stem from basic principles of humanity and compassion.

Cultural Perspectives: Is Common-Sense Universal?

Common-sense often varies across cultures, influenced by traditions, norms, and shared values.

1. Western vs. Eastern Approaches:

In Western cultures, common-sense emphasises individualism and critical thinking. In contrast, Eastern cultures often integrate collective wisdom and harmony into their version of common-sense.

Example:

In Japan, the principle of *kaizen* (continuous improvement) reflects a cultural manifestation of common-sense. By consistently seeking small, practical changes, Japanese organisations like Toyota revolutionised industries. This principle underscores how common-sense can adapt to cultural priorities.

2. Global Context:

While the expression of common-sense differs, its essence—a reliance on practical judgement—is universal. The variations remind us that common-sense is shaped by context and environment.

Practical Tip:

When working in multicultural settings, take time to understand the cultural underpinnings of common-sense. What seems "obvious" to you may differ for someone from another background.

Psychological Perspectives: The Science Behind Common-Sense

Psychologists view common-sense as a blend of cognitive and emotional intelligence.

1. Cognitive Aspect:

Common-sense involves pattern recognition and applying past experiences to current situations. It relies on the brain's ability to process information efficiently and reach practical conclusions.

Example:

Dr. APJ Abdul Kalam, India's "Missile Man," exemplified common-sense in his scientific pursuits. Despite working in complex fields, he often stressed the importance of practical applications, ensuring his innovations served society. His blend of scientific knowledge and common-sense led to breakthroughs that transformed lives.

2. Emotional Intelligence:

Empathy and self-awareness are integral to common-sense. Understanding people's needs and emotions allows for sound decision-making.

Example:

Indra Nooyi, former CEO of PepsiCo, balanced corporate success with empathy. Her common-sense approach to leadership included writing personal letters to employees' families, recognising the role of emotional intelligence in fostering loyalty and motivation.

Comparing Common-Sense with Intuition, Logic, and Wisdom

Common-sense often overlaps with intuition, logic, and wisdom, but they are distinct concepts.

1. Intuition vs. Common-Sense:

Intuition is a gut feeling—a subconscious insight often based on experience. Common-sense, on the other hand, requires conscious reasoning.

Example:

Dhirubhai Ambani, founder of Reliance Industries, relied on common-sense when identifying market opportunities. While intuition may have sparked ideas, his decisions were rooted in practical, calculated judgement, ensuring success in a competitive environment.

2. Logic vs. Common-Sense:

Logic is systematic and rules-based, while common-sense is situational and adaptable.

Example:

During the Cuban Missile Crisis, U.S. President John F. Kennedy demonstrated common-sense by choosing diplomacy over aggression. While logic suggested a military response, his practical judgement avoided a catastrophic war.

3. Wisdom vs. Common-Sense:

Wisdom encompasses a broader understanding of life, often acquired over time. Common-sense is its actionable counterpart, focused on immediate, practical solutions.

Example:

Ratan Tata displayed wisdom in long-term planning but relied on common-sense for decisions like launching affordable cars or rebranding Tata Group's global image. His ability to combine wisdom and common-sense made him a visionary leader.

The Role of Experience and Exposure in Shaping Common-Sense

Common-sense is not purely innate; it is cultivated through life experiences and exposure to diverse perspectives.

1. Learning from Failure:

Failures often teach valuable lessons, enhancing practical judgement.

Example:

Colonel Harland Sanders, the founder of KFC, faced numerous rejections before perfecting his chicken recipe. His common-sense approach—focusing on flavour and consistency—turned a small roadside business into a global empire.

2. Exposure to Diversity:

Interacting with different cultures, professions, and environments broadens one's understanding of practical solutions.

Example:

Satya Nadella, CEO of Microsoft, emphasises empathy and curiosity as key leadership traits. His exposure to diverse teams and global challenges shaped his common-sense approach to corporate transformation.

3. Mentorship and Guidance:

Learning from mentors can accelerate the development of common-sense.

Example:

Narendra Modi, India's Prime Minister, often credits his early life experiences and mentors for shaping his pragmatic leadership style. His common-sense initiatives, like promoting cleanliness through the Swachh Bharat Abhiyan, have had a tangible, widespread impact.

Practical Tips for Cultivating Common-Sense

1. Reflect . Experiences:

Regularly analyse your successes and failures. Ask: *What worked? What didn't? Why?*

2. Stay Curious:

Explore new ideas and perspectives. Curiosity broadens understanding and sharpens judgement.

3. Simplify Decisions:

Break down complex problems into smaller, manageable parts. Focus on practical, actionable steps.

4. Seek Feedback:

Encourage honest feedback from peers and mentors. Constructive criticism enhances decision-making skills.

5. Practice Empathy:

Understand others' needs and emotions before making decisions. Empathy adds depth to common-sense.

Conclusion

Common-sense is not a mystical gift; it is a skill that can be nurtured through experience, reflection, and practice. By understanding its nuances and distinctions, we can unlock its potential to navigate life's complexities with clarity and confidence.

> *"Common-sense is not about knowing the answer;*
> *it's about knowing the next best step."*
> *– Ankur*

Reflection Questions

1. How do you differentiate between intuition, logic, and common-sense in your decision-making?

2. Can you recall a situation where you used—or failed to use—common-sense? What was the outcome?

3. How has your cultural or personal background influenced your understanding of common-sense?

Plan of Action

1. Analyse Decisions:

For the next week, consciously review one decision daily. Identify if and how common-sense played a role.

2. Embrace New Experiences:

Engage in an activity or interaction outside your comfort zone. Reflect on how it challenges or reinforces your judgement.

3. Mentorship Check-in:

Identify a mentor or role model known for their practical wisdom. Seek their insights on cultivating common-sense.

By consciously integrating common-sense into our daily lives, we can make decisions that are not only practical but also profoundly impactful.

Chapter 3

The Pillars of Common-Sense

*"The ability to observe without evaluating is
the highest form of intelligence."
– Jiddu Krishnamurti*

Common-sense, while seemingly simple, is underpinned by foundational skills that guide decision-making and problem-solving.

These pillars—observation, critical thinking, and awareness—form the bedrock of practical judgement. Each pillar strengthens our ability to perceive, process, and respond to situations with clarity and effectiveness. In this chapter, we'll explore how these elements contribute to common-sense and see how successful individuals have harnessed these skills.

Pillar 1: Observation – Seeing Reality Clearly

Observation is more than just looking; it's the ability to notice details, patterns, and nuances in people, situations, and the environment. It's the first step toward developing common-sense, as it enables us to base decisions on reality rather than assumptions.

Why Observation Matters

1. Understanding Context:

Observation helps us grasp the broader context of a situation, ensuring decisions are informed by the bigger picture.

2. Recognising Patterns:

By observing repeated behaviours or trends, we can predict outcomes and make proactive decisions.

Example:

Steve Jobs was a master observer. His keen attention to how people interacted with technology led to innovations like the iPhone. Jobs didn't merely rely on market research; he observed human behaviour and identified unspoken needs, such as the desire for an intuitive interface.

How to Cultivate Observation Skills

1. Practice Mindful Observation:

Dedicate time to focus on your surroundings without distractions. Notice details you usually overlook.

2. Ask Questions:

Why is something happening? What factors contribute to it? Questions sharpen your ability to discern meaningful insights.

3. Keep a Journal:

Document daily observations. Over time, patterns will emerge, refining your judgement.

Ratan Tata's decision to develop the Tata Nano came from observing families commuting on scooters. He noticed the safety risks and the financial barriers preventing them from owning cars. His observation led to the creation of the world's most affordable car, fulfilling a significant need in the Indian market.

Pillar 2: Critical Thinking – Honing Practical Judgement

Critical thinking involves analysing information objectively and making reasoned judgements. It's about asking the right questions, identifying biases, and separating facts from opinions.

Why Critical Thinking Matters

1. Avoiding Emotional Biases:

Critical thinking ensures decisions are driven by logic rather than impulse or emotion.

2. Solving Problems Effectively:

It helps break down complex problems into manageable parts, making solutions clearer.

Example:

Dr. APJ Abdul Kalam exemplified critical thinking throughout his career. As India's "Missile Man," he approached every challenge with methodical reasoning. When faced with limited resources, Kalam prioritised innovations that had the highest impact, ensuring success despite constraints.

How to Cultivate Critical Thinking

1. Challenge Assumptions:

Don't accept information at face value. Consider alternative perspectives and question the status quo.

2. Use the 5 Whys Technique:

When faced with a problem, ask "Why?" 5 times to uncover its root cause.

3. Engage in Debates:

Discussing diverse viewpoints sharpens analytical skills and exposes cognitive blind spots.

When Indra Nooyi restructured PepsiCo, she critically evaluated the company's product portfolio. Observing global health trends, she shifted the focus to healthier snacks and beverages. Her strategic judgement ensured long-term relevance in a competitive market.

Pillar 3: Awareness – Staying Attuned to Surroundings and Emotions

Awareness bridges observation and critical thinking, enabling us to remain present and receptive to our environment and emotions. It involves understanding how external situations and internal states influence our decisions.

Why Awareness Matters

1. Enhancing Emotional Intelligence:

Awareness of emotions—both ours and others'—helps navigate interpersonal dynamics effectively.

2. Adapting to Change:

Staying aware keeps us agile, allowing us to respond swiftly to evolving circumstances.

Example:

Narendra Modi's awareness of public sentiment has been key to his leadership. From tailoring communication strategies to addressing pressing issues, his ability to gauge the nation's pulse ensures decisions resonate with the masses.

How to Cultivate Awareness

1. Practice Self-Reflection:

Regularly assess your thoughts, feelings, and actions. Awareness begins with understanding yourself.

2. Stay Present:

Focus on the current moment rather than dwelling on the past or future.

3. Seek Feedback:

Invite input from others to uncover blind spots in your awareness.

Oprah Winfrey's rise to global influence is rooted in her deep awareness of human emotions. Her ability to connect with audiences came from recognising and addressing universal struggles. Awareness enabled her to build trust and authenticity, turning her talk show into a platform for meaningful change.

Integrating the Pillars for Common-Sense

The pillars of observation, critical thinking, and awareness are interconnected. Together, they create a robust framework for applying common-sense in diverse situations.

Example of Integration:

During the 2011 tsunami in Japan, Toyota faced supply chain disruptions that could have halted production.

- **Observation:** Toyota identified bottlenecks and assessed the severity of the crisis.

- **Critical Thinking:** The company developed a prioritised recovery plan, focusing on critical components first.

- **Awareness:** Toyota considered the emotional and logistical challenges faced by employees and suppliers, ensuring empathetic leadership.

This integrated approach allowed Toyota to recover swiftly while maintaining employee morale.

Practical Tips for Strengthening the Pillars
1. For Observation:

- Observe interactions in public places.
- Notice non-verbal cues during conversations.

2. For Critical Thinking:

- Practice analysing news articles for biases.

- Solve puzzles or engage in strategic games to refine logic.

3. For Awareness:

- Meditate daily to enhance focus and emotional balance.

- Journal about daily experiences, noting emotional triggers.

Conclusion

Mastering the pillars of common-sense requires consistent effort and mindfulness. Observation allows us to see reality clearly, critical thinking sharpens our judgement, and awareness keeps us grounded and adaptable. Together, these skills transform everyday challenges into opportunities for growth and success.

> *"Common-sense is a symphony of awareness,*
> *observation, and thoughtfulness, harmonised*
> *for life's everyday challenges."*
> *– Vandana*

Reflection Questions

1. How often do you consciously observe your surroundings and the people around you?

2. When was the last time you applied critical thinking to a decision? What was the result?

3. How self-aware are you in stressful situations? How does it impact your responses?

Plan of Action

1. Daily Observation Exercise:

Spend 10 minutes each day observing your environment without distractions. Write down 3 new things you notice.

2. Critical Thinking Practice:

Choose one decision this week and analyse it using the 5 Why's technique. Document your insights.

3. Awareness Enhancement:

Start a mindfulness journal. Reflect on situations where heightened awareness could have led to better outcomes.

By integrating observation, critical thinking, and awareness into your daily life, you'll lay the groundwork for mastering common-sense—a skill as valuable as it is transformative.

Chapter 4

The Power of Simplicity

"Simplicity is the ultimate sophistication."
– Leonardo da Vinci

In a world that glorifies complexity, simplicity stands as a profound yet undervalued principle. Simplifying decisions doesn't mean oversimplifying challenges or avoiding nuance; it means cutting through the clutter to focus on what truly matters. Whether in personal life, business, or innovation, simplicity is a force multiplier for clarity, efficiency, and impact.

This chapter delves into the transformative power of simplicity, illustrated by compelling case studies of innovation and decision-making. It also provides practical tools to apply simplicity in your everyday life, demonstrating how common-sense and simplicity often go hand-in-hand.

Why Simplicity Matters

Simplicity is not just about doing less—it's about doing the right things better. It allows individuals to make more effective decisions by:

- Reducing cognitive overload.

- Sharpening the focus on priorities.

- Enhancing the ability to communicate ideas clearly.

Example: Steve Jobs and the iPhone

Steve Jobs famously believed in simplicity as a guiding principle. When Apple developed the first iPhone, Jobs insisted on a device with a single button, rejecting cluttered designs with multiple functions. This relentless focus on user-friendly design redefined smartphones, setting a standard for simplicity in technology that continues to dominate today.

Jobs's approach was rooted in common-sense—he observed how people struggled with overly complicated devices and envisioned a solution that prioritised ease of use.

Simplifying Decisions for Better Outcomes
Step 1: Identify the Core Problem

In complex situations, it's tempting to address symptoms instead of root causes. Simplifying decisions starts with asking: *What's the real issue here?*

Story:

During the Apollo 13 mission crisis, NASA faced a life-threatening problem: the spacecraft's CO_2 levels were rising dangerously. Instead of panicking over the multitude of issues caused by system failures, the engineers simplified their focus to solving the immediate problem. Using only materials available on the spacecraft, they devised a life-saving CO_2 filter.

This extraordinary success was a result of simplifying the decision-making process to address the most urgent challenge first.

Step 2: Eliminate Non-Essentials

Once the core problem is identified, cut away distractions. Simplifying often requires saying no to unnecessary elements, even if they seem appealing.

Example: Narayana Murthy and Infosys

When Infosys was founded, Narayana Murthy emphasised simplicity in its business model: delivering high-quality software services without premature diversification. By focusing on a core competency, Infosys established itself as a trusted global leader. Murthy's reliance on simplicity allowed the company to grow steadily without succumbing to the temptation of overexpansion.

Step 3: Prioritise Actionable Steps

Simplicity is about clarity in execution. Break down tasks into actionable, bite-sized steps to avoid feeling overwhelmed.

Story:

When Mahatma Gandhi initiated the Salt March, it was a simple yet powerful act of civil disobedience. Instead of overwhelming Indians with complex plans to oppose colonial rule, Gandhi chose a clear and relatable issue: reclaiming the right to produce salt. The simplicity of his strategy galvanised millions, making it one of the most effective non-violent protests in history.

Case Studies of Innovation Through Simplicity

Case Study 1: IKEA

The Swedish furniture giant IKEA revolutionised the furniture industry by simplifying its business model. Customers assemble their own furniture, which:

- Lowering manufacturing and transportation costs.

- Reduces retail prices.

- Gives consumers a sense of involvement in the process.

This innovative approach, built on simplicity, turned IKEA into a global brand that appeals to millions of cost-conscious customers.

Case Study 2: Google Search

At a time when internet search engines were cluttered with ads and multiple features, Google introduced a starkly simple homepage: a search bar and 2 buttons. This minimalist design prioritised user experience and functionality, helping Google dominate the search engine market.

Case Study 3: E-Choupal in India

ITC's E-Choupal initiative simplified agricultural supply chains in India. By introducing internet kiosks in rural areas, farmers could access real-time information about market prices, weather forecasts, and best farming practices.

The simplicity of E-Choupal's model empowered millions of farmers, increasing their income and productivity while reducing inefficiencies in the supply chain.

Practical Tips for Applying Simplicity in Daily Life

1. Declutter Your Mind:

- Practice mindfulness to focus on one task at a time.

- Maintain a to-do list with only 3-5 priorities per day.

2. Use Decision-Making Frameworks:

- Apply the Eisenhower Matrix: categorise tasks into urgent, important, and non-essential.

- Focus on high-impact, low-effort actions.

3. Simplify Communication:

- When explaining ideas, use the *"Rule of Three"*: summarise key points in 3 simple statements.

- Avoid jargon; communicate in plain language.

Example:

When Ratan Tata introduced the Tata Nano, he used simplicity not just in product design but in marketing. The car was positioned as "the people's car," emphasising affordability and utility.

The Psychological Impact of Simplicity

Simplicity also fosters psychological well-being by reducing decision fatigue. When faced with fewer choices, we're more likely to feel confident about our decisions.

Story:

Barack Obama limited his wardrobe to blue and grey suits during his presidency to simplify his morning routine. By minimising trivial decisions, he conserved mental energy for more important tasks, demonstrating the power of simplicity in leadership.

The Intersection of Common-Sense and Simplicity

Common-sense naturally gravitates toward simplicity because:

- It values practicality over perfection.
- It prioritises effectiveness over complexity.

Example:

Dabbawalas in Mumbai deliver tiffin boxes across the city with astonishing accuracy using a simple coding system. Despite the absence of sophisticated technology, their common-sense approach ensures near-perfect delivery success.

Practical Exercise: Simplicity Audit

1. Identify Complexity:

List areas in your life or work where complexity creates confusion or inefficiency.

2. Simplify Solutions:

For each area, write down one actionable step to streamline the process.

3. Implement and Reflect:

Apply the simplified solutions and evaluate the outcomes.

Conclusion

Simplicity is not a luxury; it's a necessity for making sound decisions and fostering innovation. By focusing on what truly matters, we can cut through distractions and create meaningful impact in our lives and work. As we've seen through examples like Steve Jobs, Gandhi, and IKEA, simplicity amplifies the power of common-sense.

> ***"True wisdom lies in simplifying the complex***
> ***and distilling clarity from chaos."***
> ***– Vandana***

Reflection Questions

1. In what areas of your life do you overcomplicate decisions?

2. How can you eliminate non-essential elements in your daily routines?

3. Who inspires you with their ability to simplify challenges, and what can you learn from them?

Plan of Action

1. Daily Simplification:

- Each morning, identify one task or decision to simplify.

- Use the *Eisenhower Matrix* to prioritise tasks effectively.

2. Declutter Weekly:

- Spend 30 minutes each week decluttering your workspace, digital files, or schedule.

3. Adopt a Minimalist Mindset:

- Practice the art of saying "no" to distractions or unnecessary commitments.

By embracing the power of simplicity, you unlock the potential to make smarter decisions, achieve better outcomes, and lead a life guided by clarity and purpose.

Chapter 5

Practical Decision-Making

"In every moment of decision, the best thing you
can do is the right thing, the next best thing
is the wrong thing, and the worst thing
you can do is nothing."
— Theodore Roosevelt

Making decisions is an inevitable part of life. From the mundane choices of daily routines to pivotal life-altering decisions, the process can feel overwhelming, especially in today's complex world. Yet, common-sense remains a reliable compass, helping us navigate through uncertainty with clarity and confidence.

In this chapter, we'll explore how common-sense can be applied to real-world challenges, how grounded frameworks enhance decision-making, and how some of the world's most successful individuals and organisations used common-sense to arrive at transformative solutions.

The Role of Common-Sense in Decision-Making

Common-sense bridges the gap between intuition and logic. While intuition draws from subconscious cues, and logic relies on structured reasoning, common-sense applies practical judgement rooted in context, simplicity, and relevance.

For instance, when deciding whether to invest in a business, common-sense urges you to consider its viability and relevance to the market rather than just chasing trends or hype.

The Framework for Practical Decision-Making

Effective decision-making requires a balance of speed, clarity, and grounded thinking. Here's a framework to approach decisions with common-sense:

1. Clarify the Goal:

Before deciding, define the desired outcome. A clear goal simplifies choices and aligns actions.

Example:

Indra Nooyi and PepsiCo's Transformation

As CEO of PepsiCo, Indra Nooyi observed the rising consumer shift toward healthier lifestyles. She clarified the company's goal: to transition PepsiCo into a "Performance with Purpose" brand, balancing profitability with sustainability and health-consciousness. This clarity led to innovations in product development and corporate strategy.

Practical Tip:

Ask, *What do I want to achieve? Why does it matter?* Write down your answers for clarity.

2. Gather Relevant Information:

Collect facts, insights, and perspectives that directly relate to the decision. Avoid the trap of overanalysing irrelevant details.

Example:

Ratan Tata and the Tata Nano

Ratan Tata's decision to create the Tata Nano was based on simple yet powerful observations: many Indian families commuted unsafely on two-wheelers. He gathered insights on affordability, safety, and consumer needs to create a low-cost, reliable car. Despite challenges in execution, the decision was grounded in common-sense and a genuine need.

Practical Tip:

Distinguish between "nice-to-know" and "need-to-know" information. Focus on what directly influences your decision.

3. Generate Practical Options:

Brainstorm possible solutions, emphasising practicality over perfection. Simpler options are often more effective.

Story:

The Amul Revolution

When India faced milk shortages in the 1940s, Verghese Kurien used common-sense to address the problem. He worked with local farmers to create a cooperative model that empowered them while boosting milk production. The solution—Amul—was practical, scalable, and profoundly impactful, leading to India's "White Revolution."

Practical Tip:

Frame options using a "cost-benefit analysis" lens: What's feasible, and what offers the greatest value?

4. Evaluate Risks and Rewards:

Weigh the potential benefits against risks. Common-sense urges us to neither ignore risks nor overestimate rewards but to find a balanced perspective.

Example:

Jeff Bezos and Amazon Prime

Launching Amazon Prime was a risky move for Jeff Bezos. Offering free two-day shipping could have drained profits. However, his common-sense evaluation highlighted the long-term reward: customer loyalty and increased sales. Prime became one of Amazon's most successful initiatives, proving the power of calculated risk-taking.

Practical Tip:

Ask, *What's the worst that could happen?*

What's the best?

Can I live with the downside while working toward the upside?

5. Make the Decision and Act:

Decisiveness is crucial. A decision, even imperfect, is better than none. Common-sense encourages timely action through analysis to prevent paralysis.

Story:

Dhirubhai Ambani and Reliance

Dhirubhai Ambani's decision to enter polyester manufacturing was bold but grounded in practical reasoning. Recognising India's rising textile demand, he acted decisively to build Reliance's empire. His actions were driven by common-sense: identify a growing market, understand its needs, and fulfil them efficiently.

Practical Tip:

Commit to a decision and take the first actionable step immediately.

Real-World Challenges Solved with Common-Sense
1. Elon Musk's Problem-Solving at Tesla:

When Tesla faced a production bottleneck, Elon Musk simplified the decision process: focus on improving the manufacturing line rather than over-complicating solutions. By applying straightforward engineering fixes and automating repetitive tasks, Tesla increased production efficiency, showcasing how common-sense can solve complex challenges.

2. Sudha Murty and Philanthropy:

As a philanthropist, Sudha Murty uses common-sense to evaluate the effectiveness of initiatives. Her emphasis is on practical impact rather than abstract ideals. For example, she focuses on building libraries and schools, directly addressing educational needs in underserved areas.

Lesson:

Align decisions with real-world outcomes rather than theoretical benefits.

Practical Applications of Common-Sense
1. Decision-Making in Personal Life:

- *Scenario:* Choosing between 2 job offers.

- *Common-Sense Approach:* Compare roles not just on salary but on long-term growth, work-life balance, and alignment with personal values.

2. Decision-Making in Leadership:

- *Scenario:* Introducing a new process in a team.

- *Common-Sense Approach:* Pilot the process with a small group, gather feedback, and then scale up.

3. Decision-Making in Crisis:

- *Scenario:* Managing a sudden financial setback.

- *Common-Sense Approach:* Prioritise essential expenses, communicate transparently with stakeholders, and explore practical solutions like renegotiating terms with creditors.

Tools to Enhance Practical Decision-Making
1. The 10/10/10 Rule:

Ask yourself:

- How will this decision affect me in 10 minutes?
- How will it affect me in 10 months?
- How will it affect me in 10 years?

2. The Pareto Principle (80/20 Rule):

Focus on the 20% of actions that drive 80% of results.

3. The 5-Why Method:

Identify the root cause of a problem by asking "Why?" 5 times.

Example:

A business struggling with low customer retention can uncover the root cause by asking:

1. Why are customers leaving? (Poor service quality)

2. Why is service quality poor? (Undertrained staff)

3. Why is staff undertrained? (Inadequate training resources)

4. Why are resources inadequate? (Low investment in training)

5. Why is investment low? (Misallocation of budget priorities)

Common-Sense vs. Complexity

In today's data-driven era, there's a tendency to overanalyse and complicate decisions. However, common-sense acts as an antidote, reminding us that sometimes, the simplest explanation or solution is the most effective.

Story:

Karsanbhai Patel and Nirma

Karsanbhai Patel's decision to create Nirma, an affordable detergent for Indian households, was driven by common-sense. Observing that premium detergents were unaffordable for many, he launched a product that met the market's needs at a fraction of the cost.

Conclusion

Practical decision-making is a skill that grows with intentionality and practice. By applying common-sense, leveraging frameworks, and drawing lessons from real-world examples, we can navigate challenges with confidence and clarity.

> *"Wisdom in action is common-sense*
> *made extraordinary." – Ankur*

Reflection Questions

1. How often do you rely on gut instinct versus data when making decisions?

2. Can you think of a recent decision where applying common-sense might have led to a better outcome?

3. What framework or method resonates most with your decision-making style?

Plan of Action

1. Daily Practice:

- Start small by simplifying one decision each day, such as what to eat or wear.

2. Apply Frameworks:

- Use the 10/10/10 rule or the 5-Why method to tackle bigger challenges.

3. Learn from Examples:

- Study decision-making processes of successful individuals to identify patterns.

By incorporating these strategies, you can master practical decision-making, harnessing the power of common-sense to solve real-world challenges with grace and ease.

Chapter 6

The Role of Emotional Intelligence in Common-Sense

"It is very important to understand that emotional intelligence, combined with common-sense, makes us not only smart but human."
– Daniel Goleman

Common-sense is often described as a straightforward ability to make sound judgements. However, in today's interconnected world, making wise decisions often goes beyond facts and logic— it requires emotional intelligence (EQ). EQ allows us to balance empathy with reasoning, enabling decisions that are not only practical but also humane and impactful.

In this chapter, we explore the intersection of emotional intelligence and common-sense, the role of emotional awareness in shaping wisdom, and how successful leaders and individuals have mastered this balance to achieve extraordinary outcomes.

Understanding Emotional Intelligence in the Context of Common-Sense

Emotional intelligence, as popularised by psychologist Daniel Goleman, comprises 5 key components:

1. **Self-awareness**

2. **Self-regulation**

3. **Motivation**

4. **Empathy**

5. **Social skills**

While logic and data often inform decisions, it is EQ that brings in the human factor, ensuring that choices resonate emotionally and ethically. Common-sense grounded in emotional intelligence bridges the gap between "what makes sense" and "what feels right."

Balancing Logic with Empathy

Logical decisions devoid of empathy can appear cold and disconnected, whereas empathy without logic may lead to impracticality. The art lies in balancing the 2.

Example 1: Narayana Murthy and Infosys

Narayana Murthy, the founder of Infosys, demonstrated this balance when building his company. While logic dictated strict financial discipline to scale the business, his empathy for employees led to inclusive workplace policies. His decisions were practical yet compassionate, fostering a culture of innovation and trust.

Example 2: Satya Nadella and Microsoft

Satya Nadella's leadership at Microsoft showcases the perfect marriage of logic and empathy. Upon becoming CEO, Nadella emphasised a "growth mindset," encouraging employees to learn and adapt. While he drove logical strategies to make Microsoft more competitive, his empathetic approach to understanding employee and customer needs revitalised the company culture.

Practical Tips for Balancing Logic and Empathy

1. Pause Before Acting:

When faced with decisions, take a moment to consider both the logical and emotional aspects.

2. Put Yourself in Others' Shoes:

Ask, *How will this decision affect others emotionally?*

3. Seek Diverse Perspectives:

Collaborate with others to gain insights that may challenge or expand your view.

Emotional Awareness: The Cornerstone of Practical Wisdom

What is Emotional Awareness?

Emotional awareness refers to the ability to recognise and understand your emotions and those of others. This awareness forms the foundation of practical wisdom, helping us interpret situations more holistically.

Why It Matters in Common-Sense

Without emotional awareness, decisions risk being one-dimensional, addressing surface-level concerns while ignoring deeper human factors.

Story: The Emotional Awareness of Mother Teresa

Mother Teresa's work among the poor in Kolkata was not driven by complex strategies but by her profound emotional awareness. She recognised the despair and dignity in those she served, creating initiatives that provided not just physical relief but emotional solace. Her decisions, though simple, were imbued with deep emotional wisdom.

Steps to Cultivate Emotional Awareness

1. Self-Reflection:

Spend 5-10 minutes daily journaling about your emotions and their triggers.

2. Active Listening:

When interacting with others, focus entirely on their words, tone, and body language.

3. Mindfulness Practices:

Engage in meditation or deep breathing exercises to stay present and aware of your emotions.

Using Emotional Intelligence to Enhance Common-Sense in Real Life

1. In Leadership:

Example: Ratan Tata's Leadership Style

Ratan Tata, one of India's most respected business leaders, demonstrated emotional intelligence throughout his career. When he decided to acquire Jaguar and Land Rover, his logical reasoning was supported by empathy for the struggling employees of these companies. Tata's decisions didn't just revive the brands—they fostered loyalty and admiration globally.

Lesson:

Balance financial decisions with the well-being of stakeholders.

2. In Crisis Management:

Example: Jacinda Ardern During COVID-19

New Zealand's former Prime Minister Jacinda Ardern managed the COVID-19 crisis with a remarkable combination of logic and empathy. While she implemented strict lockdowns based on scientific data, her empathetic communication—reassuring citizens and addressing their fears—built trust and compliance.

Lesson:

Empathy in communication can drive logical decisions to success.

3. In Personal Relationships:

Emotional intelligence is crucial for resolving conflicts, strengthening connections, and making thoughtful decisions in relationships.

Scenario:

You disagree with a close friend on a significant matter.

Common-Sense Approach with EQ:

1. Listen actively to their perspective without interrupting.

2. Share your viewpoint calmly, without judgement.

3. Seek common ground or agree to disagree respectfully.

Case Studies of Emotional Intelligence in Action

Case Study 1: Howard Schultz and Starbucks

Howard Schultz, the CEO of Starbucks, prioritised empathy in business decisions. When Starbucks struggled during the 2008 recession, Schultz implemented measures to preserve employee benefits like healthcare, even at the cost of short-term profits. This decision, rooted in emotional intelligence, reinforced the company's culture and loyalty, eventually contributing to its recovery.

Case Study 2: Kiran Mazumdar-Shaw and Biocon

As India's "Biotech Queen," Kiran Mazumdar-Shaw balanced emotional intelligence with innovation. She founded Biocon to make affordable healthcare accessible. Her decisions often reflected empathy for underprivileged patients while maintaining a logical focus on business sustainability.

Emotional Traps to Avoid in Decision-Making

1. Overreacting:

Strong emotions can cloud judgement. Pause before responding impulsively.

2. Ignoring Emotions:

Suppressing emotions can lead to decisions that feel hollow or unaligned with your values.

3. Over empathising:

Excessive empathy can compromise practicality. Strive for a balanced perspective.

Practical Tools for Enhancing Emotional Intelligence in Decisions

1. The Emotional-Logic Checklist:

For any decision, ask:

- *What are the facts telling me?*
- *What are my emotions telling me?*
- *What do I need to balance both?*

2. The Empathy Map:

When making decisions involving others, create an empathy map:

- *What might they be thinking?*
- *What might they be feeling?*
- *What are their needs?*

3. Journaling for Insight:

After each decision, reflect:

- What role did emotions play?

- How could I have balanced logic and empathy better?

Conclusion

Emotional intelligence is not a replacement for common-sense but an amplifier of its power. By balancing logic with empathy and cultivating emotional awareness, we can make decisions that are not only effective but also deeply meaningful.

> *"True wisdom lies in aligning the mind and heart to make decisions that resonate with both reason and compassion."*
> *– Vandana*

Reflection Questions

1. How do you currently balance logic and empathy in your decisions?

2. Can you recall a decision where emotional intelligence played a key role? What was the outcome?

3. What steps can you take to cultivate greater emotional awareness?

Plan of Action

1. Daily Practice:

Spend 5 minutes reflecting on your emotional responses to daily situations.

2. Improve Communication:

Practice active listening in every conversation, focusing on understanding the emotions behind words.

3. Use Tools:

Apply the Emotional-Logic Checklist for your next major decision.

By integrating emotional intelligence into your decisions, you can navigate life's complexities with grace, compassion, and common-sense.

Chapter 7

Common-Sense in Relationships

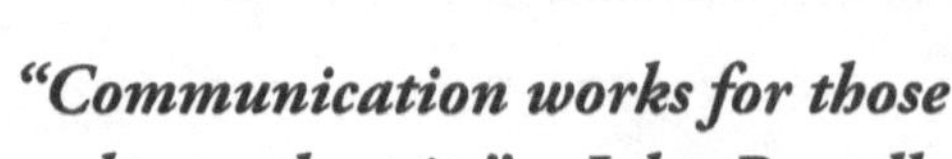

*"Communication works for those
who work at it." – John Powell*

Relationships are the bedrock of human existence, shaping who we are and how we engage with the world. Yet, maintaining healthy relationships often feels like a challenge in today's fast-paced, digital-first era. Surprisingly, many relational conflicts arise not from a lack of love or goodwill but from a deficit in applying common-sense.

This chapter delves into the role of common-sense in relationships, particularly in communication and conflict resolution.

We will also explore how everyday wisdom can build trust and respect, ensuring relationships thrive.

The Role of Common-Sense in Relationships

Common-sense in relationships is about understanding simple yet profound truths:

- People want to be heard and understood.

- Clear, honest communication is the foundation of trust.

- Conflicts are natural but can be resolved with empathy and logic.

While these principles seem straightforward, they are often overlooked in the heat of emotions or due to misunderstandings.

Communicating Effectively: The Heart of Relationship Success

The Basics of Effective Communication

At its core, effective communication involves 3 key elements:

1. **Active Listening:** Truly hearing what the other person is saying without forming responses in your head.

2. **Clarity:** Expressing your thoughts and emotions directly and respectfully.

3. **Empathy:** Understanding the other person's perspective and feelings.

Story: Ratan Tata and Communication as a Leader

Ratan Tata, one of India's most admired industrialists, is renowned for his ability to connect with people across all levels. His employees have shared countless stories of how Tata listened intently, showing empathy even in difficult situations. This practice fostered trust and loyalty within the organisation.

Lesson:

Effective communication begins with the willingness to listen without judgement.

Common-Sense Tip for Communication

- **Pause Before Responding:** When emotions run high, take a moment to breathe and organise your thoughts before replying.

Resolving Conflicts with Everyday Wisdom

Conflicts are inevitable in relationships. However, the way we approach them can either strengthen bonds or tear them apart.

The Common-Sense Approach to Conflict Resolution

1. Understand the Root Cause:

Conflicts often stem from unmet expectations or miscommunication. Identify the underlying issue before reacting.

2. Use "I" Statements:

Instead of blaming, express how you feel. For example, say, *"I feel hurt when…"* rather than *"You always…"*.

3. Seek Win-Win Solutions:

Look for compromises that respect both parties' needs and emotions.

Story: Gandhi's Approach to Resolving Conflicts

Mahatma Gandhi's philosophy of nonviolence extended to his personal relationships. He believed in resolving conflicts through dialogue and mutual respect. Whether negotiating with British leaders or resolving disputes within the Indian independence movement, Gandhi relied on listening, empathy, and a relentless commitment to fairness.

Lesson:

Resolving conflicts is about understanding the other person's viewpoint while remaining grounded in your principles.

Common-Sense Tip for Conflict Resolution

- **Pick the Right Time and Place:** Address conflicts when both parties are calm and open to discussion, not in the heat of the moment. CARE-FRONT and not CONFRONT!

Building Trust and Respect Through Everyday Wisdom

Trust and respect are earned through consistent actions, not grand gestures. Common-sense in relationships means understanding that small, everyday actions build or erode trust over time.

Three Pillars of Trust

1. **Honesty:** Always speak the truth, even when it's uncomfortable.

2. **Consistency:** Keep your promises, no matter how small.

3. **Empathy:** Show that you care about the other person's feelings and needs.

Story: The Friendship of Abdul Kalam and Arun Tiwari

Dr. APJ Abdul Kalam, India's "Missile Man," shared a profound friendship with scientist Arun Tiwari. Their relationship was built on mutual respect, trust, and shared goals. Despite their professional achievements, what stood out was their ability to support and inspire each other, even during challenging times.

Lesson:

Trust is nurtured by showing up consistently for the people who matter to you.

Common-Sense Tip for Building Trust

- **Be Reliable:** If you commit to something, follow through. Reliability strengthens relationships.

Case Studies: Common-Sense in Action
Case Study 1: Satya Nadella and Empathy in Leadership

As CEO of Microsoft, Satya Nadella transformed the company's culture by emphasising empathy and inclusion. His leadership style—rooted in listening and understanding employees' perspectives—helped Microsoft foster collaboration and innovation.

Lesson:

Empathy is a powerful tool for building trust and respect in relationships.

Case Study 2: Oprah Winfrey and Relational Wisdom

Oprah Winfrey's interviews often reveal her extraordinary ability to connect with people. Her secret? Active listening and genuine curiosity. Oprah's ability to make her guests feel heard has made her one of the most trusted media figures globally.

Lesson:

Listening attentively and asking thoughtful questions can deepen any relationship.

Common Relationship Pitfalls and How to Avoid Them

1. Assumptions:

Assuming what someone else feels or thinks often leads to misunderstandings.

Solution: Ask instead of assuming. A simple question like, *"Can you help me understand what you're feeling?"* can clear up confusion.

2. Avoidance:

Ignoring issues doesn't make them go away—it often makes them worse.

Solution: Address problems head-on, using calm and constructive language.

3. Over-Dependence on Technology:

Relying on texts or emails for serious conversations can lead to misinterpretation.

Solution: For meaningful discussions, choose face-to-face communication whenever possible.

Practical Tools for Common-Sense in Relationships

1. The 10-Second Rule:

Before reacting to a frustrating comment, count to 10. This brief pause allows emotions to settle and reason to take over.

2. Active Listening Exercise:

Practice listening to a friend or partner without interrupting. After they finish, summarise what they said to confirm your understanding.

3. Gratitude Journal:

Write down 3 things you appreciate about someone in your life each day. Share this with them periodically to strengthen your bond.

Conclusion

Common-sense in relationships isn't about grand gestures or complex strategies. It's about applying simple, timeless principles—clear communication, empathy, trustworthiness, and practical problem-solving. By bringing everyday wisdom into your interactions, you can create relationships that are not only resilient but deeply fulfilling.

"The strength of a relationship lies not in perfection,
but in the everyday acts of kindness, honesty,
and understanding that weave it together."
– Ankur

Reflection Questions

1. How often do you actively listen to the people in your life without interrupting?

2. What steps can you take to build more trust in your relationships?

3. How do you handle conflicts currently, and what could you improve?

Plan of Action

1. Daily Practice:

Dedicate 5 minutes daily to reflect on your recent interactions. Identify areas where you could have communicated more effectively.

2. Conflict Resolution:

Use the "I" statements method in your next disagreement to express your feelings without blaming.

3. Strengthen Bonds:

Make a small but meaningful gesture—like a thank-you note or an act of kindness—to show appreciation for someone in your life this week.

By incorporating common-sense into your relationships, you'll unlock the potential for deeper connections, mutual respect, and lasting harmony.

Chapter 8

Breaking Through Biases

❧

"The first principle is that you must not fool
yourself—and you are the easiest person to fool."
– Richard Feynman

Common-sense thrives in clarity, yet our minds are often clouded by biases—mental shortcuts, blind spots, and ingrained patterns of thought that distort our judgement. These biases are not just individual quirks but deeply embedded in our psychology, shaped by societal norms, cultural conditioning, and personal experiences. Breaking through these biases is essential for nurturing everyday wisdom.

This chapter explores how biases hinder common-sense, identifies the most pervasive biases, and provides practical strategies for overcoming them.

The Hidden Barriers to Common-Sense

Biases act as invisible filters, influencing our decisions and perceptions without our awareness. Recognising these barriers is the first step toward cultivating clearer, unbiased thinking.

Story: The Challenger Disaster and Groupthink

In 1986, NASA's Challenger space shuttle exploded shortly after take-off, killing all 7 astronauts on board. Investigations revealed that engineers had warned about potential technical issues with the O-ring seals, but their concerns were dismissed in the decision-making process. Groupthink—where the desire for consensus overrides individual judgement—was a significant contributor to the tragedy.

Lesson:

Biases like groupthink can have catastrophic consequences. Breaking through them requires fostering an environment where diverse opinions are encouraged and valued.

Recognising and Addressing Mental Blind Spots
The Science of Bias

Cognitive biases are shortcuts our brains use to simplify decision-making. While they save time and effort, they often lead us astray by prioritising convenience over accuracy.

Types of Mental Blind Spots

1. **Confirmation Bias:** Seeking information that supports our preexisting beliefs while ignoring contradictory evidence.

2. **Anchoring Bias:** Relying too heavily on the first piece of information encountered.

3. **Status Quo Bias:** Preferring the familiar and resisting change, even when alternatives may be better.

Practical Tips to Overcome Blind Spots

1. **Seek Contradictory Information:** Actively look for evidence that challenges your assumptions.

2. **Delay Judgements:** Take time to gather and analyse information before making decisions.

3. **Invite Diverse Perspectives:** Engage with people who have different viewpoints or experiences.

Tackling Confirmation Bias: Seeing Beyond Your Beliefs

What Is Confirmation Bias?

Confirmation bias is the tendency to interpret new information in a way that confirms our existing beliefs. This bias is prevalent in personal decisions, workplace dynamics, and even societal debates.

Story: Dhirubhai Ambani's Unbiased Vision

Dhirubhai Ambani, the founder of Reliance Industries, succeeded by challenging conventional wisdom and embracing contradictory perspectives. In the 1970s, when sceptics doubted India's potential for large-scale industrialisation, Ambani sought data and insights that proved otherwise. His ability to see beyond biases laid the foundation for one of India's largest conglomerates.

Lesson:

Breaking confirmation bias involves being open to ideas that challenge your worldview and exploring possibilities that others may dismiss.

Practical Tips for Tackling Confirmation Bias

1. **Ask "What If?" Questions:** What if your belief is wrong? What alternatives might exist?

2. **Engage with Opposing Viewpoints:** Read, watch, or listen to content that contradicts your assumptions.

3. **Adopt a Beginner's Mindset:** Approach situations with curiosity, as if learning about them for the first time.

Confronting Groupthink: Valuing Individual Judgement
The Pitfalls of Groupthink

Groupthink occurs when the desire for harmony in a group leads to poor decision-making. It suppresses dissenting opinions, creating an illusion of consensus.

Story: Elon Musk's Bold Independence

Elon Musk is known for challenging groupthink in industries ranging from space exploration to electric vehicles. When critics dismissed the viability of Tesla, Musk relied on his independent judgement and data-driven analysis to push forward. His ability to think critically and defy popular opinion has revolutionised multiple industries.

Lesson:

Avoiding groupthink requires courage to stand apart from the crowd and trust your reasoned conclusions.

Practical Tips for Combating Groupthink

1. **Encourage Dissent:** Foster an environment where questioning and constructive criticism are welcomed.

2. **Appoint a Devil's Advocate:** Assign someone to challenge assumptions and highlight potential flaws in decisions.

3. **Conduct Anonymous Polls:** Gather honest feedback without the pressure of group dynamics.

Cultural Conditioning: Seeing Beyond Social Norms
The Role of Culture in Shaping Biases

Cultural norms and traditions shape our thinking, often unconsciously. While these norms provide structure, they can also restrict independent thought and perpetuate outdated beliefs.

Story: Verghese Kurien and the Milk Revolution

Verghese Kurien, the father of India's White Revolution, broke through cultural biases that dismissed small-scale dairy farmers as incapable of large-scale success. By challenging these assumptions, Kurien empowered rural communities, transforming India into the world's largest producer of milk.

Lesson:

Cultural conditioning can limit potential, but questioning norms with practical reasoning can lead to groundbreaking achievements.

Practical Tips for Breaking Cultural Biases

1. **Question Traditional Beliefs:** Ask whether long-held norms are relevant and beneficial today.

2. **Learn from Other Cultures:** Expose yourself to diverse practices and philosophies to gain broader perspectives.

3. **Focus on Principles, Not Practices:** Understand the underlying values of traditions, and adapt them to modern contexts.

Building a Bias-Free Mindset

Step 1: Self-Awareness

Recognise your biases by reflecting on your beliefs and decisions.

Exercise:

Write down a recent decision and identify any biases that may have influenced it.

Step 2: Critical Thinking

Challenge assumptions by analysing information objectively.

Exercise:

For any opinion you hold strongly, list arguments against it.

Step 3: Feedback

Invite honest feedback from trusted individuals to uncover blind spots.

Exercise:

Ask a mentor or colleague to critique your reasoning on a specific issue.

Case Studies: Breaking Through Biases
Case Study 1: Mahatma Gandhi's Empathy for All

Gandhi overcame cultural biases by advocating for unity among diverse communities. His ability to see beyond societal divisions was rooted in his common-sense approach to understanding human nature.

Lesson:

Breaking biases requires empathy and a commitment to universal values.

Case Study 2: Steve Jobs and Simplicity in Innovation

Steve Jobs challenged the complexity bias in technology by focusing on simplicity. His ability to strip away unnecessary features and focus on user-friendly design transformed Apple into an industry leader.

Lesson:

Simplicity is a powerful antidote to the bias of overcomplication.

Conclusion

Breaking through biases is an essential step in mastering common-sense. By recognising mental blind spots, questioning ingrained beliefs, and fostering critical thinking, we can achieve clearer, more grounded decision-making. Everyday wisdom is not about rejecting all biases but learning to identify and navigate them with intention and awareness.

"True wisdom lies not in knowing everything, but in questioning everything—and having the courage to change what doesn't make sense." – Vandana

Reflection Questions

1. What biases have influenced your decisions recently?

2. How can you actively challenge groupthink in your professional or personal life?

3. What cultural norms or beliefs might be limiting your perspective?

Plan of Action

1. **Bias Journal:** Start a journal to record decisions and identify potential biases influencing them.

2. **Engage in Diverse Conversations:** Actively seek dialogue with people from different cultural, professional, or ideological backgrounds.

3. **Practice Dissent:** In group discussions, play the role of devil's advocate to challenge assumptions and promote critical thinking.

By addressing biases with self-awareness and deliberate action, you'll unlock the full potential of your common-sense, enabling you to navigate life's complexities with clarity and confidence.

Chapter 9

Dealing with Information Overload

*"The ability to simplify means to eliminate
the unnecessary so that the necessary may speak."*
– Hans Hofmann

In a world driven by technology and endless streams of data, information overload has become one of the greatest barriers to common-sense. Each day, we are bombarded with news, emails, messages, and social media updates, leaving little room for clarity and critical thinking. This overwhelming influx of information can cloud judgement, hinder decision-making, and distance us from the essence of common-sense.

This chapter explores how to navigate the era of information overload by filtering noise, focusing on the essential, and employing strategies for critical thinking in a data-driven world.

The Paradox of Too Much Information

Information overload occurs when the sheer volume of available information exceeds our cognitive capacity to process it effectively. While access to information is vital, too much of it leads to confusion, inaction, and a diminished ability to prioritise what truly matters.

Story: Warren Buffett and the Power of Focus

Warren Buffett, one of the world's most successful investors, is known for his ability to cut through noise and focus on what's essential. Buffett once shared that his success comes not from reading everything but from selectively choosing what adds value. He famously reads 500 pages a day but emphasises quality over quantity, focusing on material that sharpens his investment decisions.

Lesson:

Navigating information overload requires the discipline to prioritise and filter only what aligns with your goals.

The Impact of Noise on Common-Sense

How Noise Affects Decision-Making

1. **Analysis Paralysis:** With too much information, making decisions becomes overwhelming.

2. **Loss of Clarity:** Key insights get buried under irrelevant details.

3. **Stress and Burnout:** Constant exposure to information overload leads to mental fatigue.

Story: The Mars Climate Orbiter Failure

In 1999, NASA's Mars Climate Orbiter mission failed due to a mix-up between metric and imperial units. The critical error was buried under layers of communication and technical data, highlighting how unfiltered information can obscure vital details.

Lesson:

Even in high-stakes environments, failing to filter and focus on essential information can lead to disastrous outcomes.

Filtering Noise: The Art of Prioritisation

1. Define Your Objectives:

Knowing what you want to achieve is the first step in filtering noise. Clear goals act as a lens through which you can evaluate the relevance of incoming information.

Practical Tip:

Write down your top 3 priorities for the day. Use these as a guide to assess whether the information you consume aligns with your objectives.

2. Limit Your Inputs:

Reduce the number of sources you consume daily. Instead of browsing dozens of websites or social media platforms, focus on a few trusted ones.

Practical Tip:

Unsubscribe from unnecessary newsletters and turn off non-essential notifications.

3. Use Technology Wisely:

Tools like RSS feeds, curated newsletters, or reading apps can help consolidate and organise information.

Practical Tip:

Use apps like Pocket or Feedly to save articles and read them during dedicated time slots, avoiding constant interruptions.

Focusing on the Essential: Strategies for Simplification

1. Apply the 80/20 Rule:

The Pareto Principle states that 80% of outcomes come from 20% of efforts. Identify the 20% of information that drives the majority of value in your decisions.

Story: Steve Jobs and Apple's Simplified Product Line

When Steve Jobs returned to Apple in 1997, the company was struggling with a cluttered product lineup. Jobs applied the 80/20 rule by cutting down Apple's offerings to just a handful of high-quality products. This focus not only streamlined operations but also propelled Apple to unprecedented success.

Lesson:

Simplifying choices allows you to focus on what truly matters, enhancing clarity and efficiency.

2. Use Decision Frameworks:

Frameworks like Eisenhower's Matrix or the Rule of Three can help you prioritise tasks and information effectively.

Eisenhower's Matrix:

- Urgent and important: Do it immediately.
- Important but not urgent: Schedule it.

- Urgent but not important: Delegate it.
- Neither urgent nor important: Eliminate it.

3. Practice Mindfulness:

Mindfulness helps you stay present and discern between what is useful and what is distracting.

Practical Tip:

Before consuming information, take a moment to ask: "Is this helping me move closer to my goals?"

Critical Thinking in a Data-Driven World

Critical thinking is the antidote to information overload. It enables you to evaluate, analyse, and use information effectively, rather than being overwhelmed by it.

1. Evaluate the Source:

Not all information is created equal. Assess the credibility of sources by checking their expertise, track record, and objectivity.

Practical Tip:

Ask yourself: "Is this source reliable? What is their motive in sharing this information?"

2. Distinguish Between Facts and Opinions:

Many opinions are presented as facts, especially in the age of social media. Developing the ability to separate the 2 is crucial for sound judgement.

Story: Ratan Tata and Rational Thinking

Ratan Tata, one of India's most respected industrialists, often relied on critical thinking to navigate complex business decisions. When launching the Tata Nano, he analysed customer needs and market dynamics rather than being swayed by critics' opinions. This pragmatic approach led to innovation tailored to real-world challenges.

Lesson:

Focusing on facts over opinions enables practical and impactful decision-making.

3. Question Assumptions:

Challenge the underlying assumptions of any information you encounter. This helps uncover biases or gaps in reasoning.

Practical Tip:

Ask: "What evidence supports this? What evidence contradicts it?"

Case Studies: Success in Simplifying and Filtering
Case Study 1: Marie Kondo's Method of Decluttering

Marie Kondo's Kon Mari method teaches people to declutter their homes by keeping only items that "spark joy." Her approach to physical spaces mirrors the mental process of filtering noise—focusing only on what truly matters.

Lesson:

Eliminating unnecessary clutter, whether physical or informational, creates room for clarity and purpose.

Case Study 2: Barack Obama's Decision-Making Style

As U.S. President, Barack Obama simplified his daily routine by limiting trivial decisions. He wore only grey or blue suits to conserve decision-making energy for critical issues.

Lesson:

Simplifying routine choices frees cognitive resources for higher-value decisions.

Conclusion

Dealing with information overload is not about rejecting information but about mastering the art of filtering and focusing. By defining priorities, applying critical thinking, and embracing simplicity, you can break free from the noise and make decisions rooted in common-sense.

> ***"Wisdom is not in knowing more;***
> ***it's in knowing what to ignore."***
> *— Vandana*

Reflection Questions

1. What are the primary sources of information that overwhelm you?

2. How can you simplify your daily choices to focus on what truly matters?

3. In what ways can you cultivate critical thinking to navigate data-driven challenges?

Plan of Action

1. **Audit Your Information Diet:** List all the sources of information you consume daily. Eliminate those that do not align with your priorities.

2. **Create a Focus Routine:** Set specific times for consuming information and stick to them. Avoid multitasking.

3. **Practice the 3-Question Filter:** For any new information, ask:

   - Is it relevant to my goals?

   - Is it credible and factual?

   - How can I use it effectively?

By taming information overload, you reclaim the clarity and focus needed to harness your common-sense and thrive in today's complex world.

Chapter 10

The Courage to Be Practical

*"Practicality is not the enemy of innovation;
it's the foundation of achievement."*
– Ankur

In a world where trends, hype, and complexity dominate the narrative, practicality often takes a backseat. Embracing practicality requires courage—a willingness to step away from the noise, trust one's judgement, and make decisions grounded in reality. This chapter delves into the power of practicality, exploring stories of individuals who prioritised common-sense over trends and demonstrating how practical decisions lead to lasting success.

Why Is Practicality Undervalued?

The allure of complexity often overshadows the value of practical solutions. We live in an era where sophisticated ideas are glorified, and simplicity is sometimes mistaken for a lack of ambition. Yet, the most successful people understand that practicality is not a compromise; it's a pathway to clarity and effectiveness.

The Role of Trends in Clouding Judgement

From fashion to technology to business strategies, trends can steer decisions away from practicality. People often follow trends to fit in or appear innovative, even when such choices are ill-suited to their circumstances.

Story: Nokia's Downfall

Once a global leader in mobile phones, Nokia lost its dominance by ignoring practical market trends like the shift to smartphones. Instead of adapting to consumer demands, it clung to its existing technology, eventually losing relevance.

Lesson:

Practicality requires aligning decisions with real-world needs, not clinging to outdated methods or blindly following trends.

The Fear of Being Ordinary

In a society that celebrates innovation and disruption, practicality can feel like settling for mediocrity. However, it takes courage to focus on what works rather than chasing what's fashionable.

Story: Amul's Practical Approach to Growth

Amul, India's leading dairy cooperative, built its success on a simple, practical model: empowering farmers and creating a reliable supply chain. Instead of chasing global trends or diversifying excessively, Amul focused on delivering quality dairy products at scale.

Lesson:

By prioritising practical solutions, Amul achieved sustained growth and became a household name.

The Core Principles of Practicality

Practicality is not a rejection of ambition; it's a way to channel ambition into actionable and achievable steps.

1. Focus on the Outcome:

Practicality involves keeping the end goal in sight and aligning every action toward achieving it. This requires clarity of purpose and a willingness to adapt.

Practical Tip:

Before making a decision, ask yourself: *Does this move me closer to my goal?*

2. Simplify Complexity:

Simplifying complex problems doesn't mean ignoring their nuances; it means breaking them down into manageable parts.

Story: Elon Musk's First Principles Thinking

Elon Musk often uses "first principles" to simplify decision-making. When working on Tesla's battery design, Musk analysed the core materials' costs and processes, leading to significant cost reductions.

Lesson:

Simplicity can drive groundbreaking solutions without compromising on innovation.

3. Balance Ambition with Feasibility:

Practicality doesn't mean shunning big dreams; it means pursuing them with a realistic approach.

Practical Tip:

Set SMART goals—Specific, Measurable, Achievable, Relevant, and Time-bound—to ensure your ambitions are grounded in practicality.

Stories of Courageous Practicality

The following examples illustrate how individuals used common-sense and practicality to overcome challenges and achieve remarkable results.

1. Indra Nooyi: Practical Leadership at PepsiCo:

As the CEO of PepsiCo, Indra Nooyi demonstrated the courage to balance profitability with sustainability. Recognising the growing demand for healthier options, she introduced low-sugar and low-calorie products while maintaining the company's iconic offerings.

Practical Move:

Instead of abandoning traditional products or jumping on extreme health trends, Nooyi took a balanced approach, aligning PepsiCo's strategy with consumer preferences.

Lesson:

Practicality lies in understanding the middle ground between innovation and continuity.

2. E. Sreedharan: The Metro Man of India:

E. Sreedharan led the construction of the Delhi Metro, one of India's most ambitious infrastructure projects. Despite budget constraints, political interference, and logistical challenges, he completed the project on time and within budget.

Practical Move:

Sreedharan emphasised meticulous planning, accountability, and resource optimisation.

Lesson:

Practicality, coupled with discipline, can transform seemingly impossible goals into reality.

3. Rosa Parks: A Practical Stand Against Injustice:

Rosa Parks' decision to refuse giving up her bus seat was not just an act of defiance; it was a calculated, practical move to ignite the civil rights movement.

Practical Move:

Her action was part of a broader strategy that relied on the collective power of her community.

Lesson:

Practicality can be a powerful tool for driving social change when combined with courage and intention.

Practical Decision-Making in Action

Practicality is a skill that can be cultivated through conscious effort.

1. Start with Reality:

Accept the current situation without embellishment or denial. Practical decisions are rooted in a clear understanding of what is, not what could be.

Practical Tip:

Conduct a SWOT analysis (Strengths, Weaknesses, Opportunities, Threats) to assess your reality before making decisions.

2. Embrace Incremental Progress:

Instead of attempting massive leaps, focus on small, consistent steps.

Story: Dabbawalas of Mumbai

Mumbai's dabbawalas deliver home-cooked meals across the city with astonishing precision, using a simple yet effective system of codes and teamwork.

Practical Move:

By relying on tried-and-tested methods rather than high-tech solutions, they achieve a Six Sigma level of efficiency.

Lesson:

Consistency in small actions often yields extraordinary results.

3. Adapt to Feedback:

Practicality involves staying flexible and refining decisions based on outcomes and new information.

Practical Tip:

Use feedback loops to assess what's working and pivot when necessary.

Overcoming Barriers to Practicality

Several barriers can hinder practical decision-making, but awareness and intentional action can help overcome them.

1. Emotional Bias:

Emotions often cloud judgement, leading to impractical decisions.

Practical Tip:

Pause and assess your emotional state before making critical decisions. Use techniques like journaling or meditation to gain clarity.

2. Fear of Judgement:

The fear of appearing unoriginal or unambitious can deter people from practical choices.

Practical Tip:

Remind yourself that practicality often leads to long-term respect and success, even if it seems unglamorous initially.

3. Lack of Confidence:

Believing that practical decisions are "too simple" can undermine confidence in their effectiveness.

Story: APJ Abdul Kalam's Vision for Rural India

APJ Abdul Kalam advocated for practical, scalable solutions to uplift rural India, such as solar power and low-cost technology. His confidence in simple ideas led to transformative change.

Lesson:

Practical decisions require conviction in their impact, no matter how small they seem.

Conclusion

In a world obsessed with complexity and trends, practicality stands as a beacon of clarity and purpose. It takes courage to prioritise common-sense, embrace simplicity, and make decisions grounded in reality. The stories and strategies in this chapter demonstrate that practical thinking is not only a skill but also a mindset—one that leads to meaningful, lasting outcomes.

> *"Greatness isn't about grand gestures;*
> *it's about practical actions taken consistently."*
> *– Vandana*

Reflection Questions

1. What recent decision could you have approached more practically?

2. How can you simplify your approach to a current challenge?

3. What steps can you take to embrace practicality in your daily life?

Plan of Action

1. **Define Practical Goals:** Write down one area where practicality can improve your outcomes.

2. **Simplify Processes:** Identify one complex process in your life and break it into actionable steps.

3. **Act Consistently:** Choose one small, practical action to take every day for the next week, and track its impact.

By embracing practicality, you'll discover that common-sense is not just a skill but a powerful force for success and fulfilment.

Chapter 11

Observation:
The Gateway to Wisdom

*"The ability to observe is the foundation
of all wisdom. Without observation, we are lost in
the noise of the world."*
– Vandana

In a world where distractions are constant and attention spans are short, the art of observation has become a rare skill. Yet, it is perhaps one of the most valuable tools for gaining wisdom. Observation allows us to understand the world clearly, learn from our surroundings, and make informed decisions. In this chapter, we will explore how sharpening our observation skills can unlock wisdom and guide us toward better decision-making, and how mindfulness plays a crucial role in cultivating clear perception.

Why Observation Matters

Observation is not just about seeing; it's about perceiving. It's about paying attention to details, noticing patterns, and understanding what is happening beneath the surface. In an age of overwhelming information and constant stimuli, the ability to observe with clarity is more important than ever. It enables us to navigate through complexity and find meaningful insights that others might overlook.

The most successful individuals across various fields—whether in business, art, or even day-to-day life—share one thing in common: they are exceptional observers. They notice things others miss, and this heightened awareness often leads them to make decisions that are grounded in reality, not assumptions.

The Power of Observation in Everyday Life

To understand how powerful observation can be, let's explore how different individuals have used it to their advantage in real-life situations.

Story: Steve Jobs and the Power of Observation

Steve Jobs, the co-founder of Apple, was known for his extraordinary attention to detail. Jobs was not only a visionary but also an exceptional observer of people, products, and trends. He often attributed much of Apple's success to his ability to observe the needs of customers, anticipate future trends, and understand the user experience. Jobs famously noticed how people were frustrated with the complexity of existing mobile devices and set out to create an iPhone that would be simple, intuitive, and user-friendly.

Lesson:

By observing the frustrations of others, Jobs revolutionised the tech industry. Observation can uncover opportunities where others see only problems.

Story: Mahatma Gandhi and His Keen Sense of Observation

Mahatma Gandhi, the leader of India's non-violent independence movement, used keen observation to deeply understand the struggles of the Indian people. His ability to observe not only the socio-political landscape but also the everyday lives of individuals in rural India led him to realise the importance of self-sufficiency and the need for a simple, sustainable lifestyle. His observation of British colonial rule's impact on India shaped his actions, such as the Salt March, a peaceful protest against British taxation.

Lesson:

Gandhi's wisdom came from observing the small, often overlooked details that others dismissed. Observation, when combined with empathy, leads to profound insight and action.

Techniques for Strengthening Observation Skills

Observation is a skill that can be developed with practice. By honing your ability to observe clearly and effectively, you can gain insights that lead to better decisions and wiser choices. Below are some techniques that can help sharpen your observation skills:

1. Slow Down and Be Present:

In our fast-paced world, it's easy to rush through life without truly noticing what's happening around us. To become a better observer, we must first slow down. Take the time to be present and engage with your environment rather than simply passing through it. When you're walking in nature, for example, instead of rushing to your destination, pause and take note of the sounds, colours, and smells around you. This simple act of slowing down allows your brain to take in more information and process it more effectively.

Practical Tip:

Spend 5 minutes each day simply observing your surroundings without any distractions. Take note of the smallest details—whether it's the way light filters through the trees or the subtle shift in a person's expression.

2. Practice Active Listening:

A key component of observation is listening—truly listening. Active listening means fully engaging with the speaker, focusing on not just their words but also their tone, body language, and underlying emotions. By tuning into these subtle cues, you can gain a deeper understanding of what is really being communicated.

Story: Oprah Winfrey's Active Listening

Oprah Winfrey, one of the most successful talk show hosts in history, is known for her ability to listen deeply. She has an uncanny ability to read between the lines of what her guests are saying and respond in a way that brings out their true feelings. Oprah's success in connecting with people on a personal level is largely attributed to her acute observation and active listening skills.

Lesson:

Active listening not only helps you understand others but also enhances your ability to perceive the nuances in their emotions and intentions.

3. Observe Patterns, Not Just Events:

Being observant means looking beyond the surface. Rather than just noticing isolated incidents or singular events, ask yourself: *What patterns can I observe here?* Patterns are key to understanding behaviours, predicting outcomes, and finding solutions to complex problems.

Story: J.K. Rowling and Observing Human Nature

J.K. Rowling, the author of the Harry Potter series, often attributes the success of her books to her ability to observe human behaviour. She took inspiration from real-life personalities and everyday encounters to create rich, multi-faceted characters. The relationships and conflicts in the Harry Potter series mirror the complexities of the human experience, and this level of understanding came from Rowling's deep observations of people.

Lesson:

By noticing recurring patterns in behaviour, you can gain valuable insights into people's motivations and actions, which can inform your decisions and strategies.

4. Ask the Right Questions:

Asking insightful questions is a powerful tool for improving your observation skills. Instead of simply accepting things at face value, ask yourself deeper questions about what you're seeing. What is the motivation behind this action? Why is someone behaving this way? What's the underlying cause of this issue? These questions help you go beyond superficial observation and uncover hidden truths.

Practical Tip:

Whenever you observe something, make it a habit to ask "Why?" 5 times. This technique, known as the "Five Whys," encourages you to dig deeper into the root causes of what you're seeing.

5. Use Mindfulness to Enhance Perception:

Mindfulness is the practice of paying full attention to the present moment without judgement. It is a powerful tool for enhancing observation because it trains your mind to be fully engaged with your surroundings. Mindfulness enables you to notice even the smallest details and helps you observe without being clouded by preconceived notions or biases.

Story: The Mindfulness of a Great Chef

Great chefs, such as René Redzepi of Noma, the world-renowned restaurant in Copenhagen, emphasise mindfulness in their approach to cooking. Redzepi often speaks about how the act of cooking is not just about following a recipe but observing the ingredients, the seasons, and the nuances of flavour. This mindfulness allows chefs to create extraordinary dishes that go beyond mere sustenance, turning food into art.

Lesson:

By practicing mindfulness, you can refine your ability to observe not just the obvious but also the subtle, allowing you to make decisions that are informed by a deeper understanding.

The Role of Mindfulness in Clear Perception

Mindfulness is not just a practice for relaxation—it is a powerful tool for improving clarity of perception. In order to observe the world around us with clarity, we need to silence the noise in our minds and focus on what is in front of us. Mindfulness helps us clear away distractions, allowing us to perceive things as they are, without bias or judgement.

1. Mindfulness Enhances Emotional Awareness:

One of the key aspects of mindfulness is emotional awareness. When we are mindful, we become more aware of our emotions and how they influence our perceptions. For example, if we are angry or frustrated, we may interpret situations in a biased way. Mindfulness helps us recognise and regulate these emotions, enabling us to observe our surroundings with greater objectivity.

Practical Tip:

Practice deep breathing exercises when you feel emotionally charged. This will help you regain control and observe the situation with a calm and clear mind.

2. Mindfulness Improves Focus and Attention:

In today's world, distractions are everywhere—smartphones, social media, and constant notifications. Mindfulness helps improve our ability to focus and pay attention to what truly matters. When we are fully engaged with the present moment, we can observe things with greater precision, which ultimately leads to better decision-making.

Story: The Focused Mind of Albert Einstein

Albert Einstein, one of the greatest minds in history, was known for his deep focus and mindfulness in his work. He would often retreat to quiet spaces to think through complex problems, giving himself the time and mental clarity to observe patterns that others missed. His ability to observe and think deeply led to groundbreaking theories that changed the world.

Lesson:

Mindfulness is essential for developing the kind of deep, focused observation that leads to true insight.

Conclusion

Observation is more than just seeing; it's about perceiving, understanding, and uncovering the truth beneath the surface. By cultivating strong observation skills and integrating mindfulness into our lives, we can unlock wisdom and make decisions grounded in clarity. Observation empowers us to navigate the complexities of the world, notice patterns, and discover solutions that are hidden in plain sight.

> *"Observation is the gateway to wisdom,*
> *for it is through what we see and perceive that*
> *we truly understand the world."*
> *— Vandana*

Reflection Questions

1. How can you improve your ability to observe in your daily life?

2. What are some patterns you have overlooked in your current situation?

3. How can mindfulness improve your perception in both personal and professional contexts?

By practicing mindfulness and observation, we open the door to greater wisdom, creating a clear path forward in life.

Chapter 12

Critical Thinking as a Lifelong Habit

⸺❦❦⸺

*"Critical thinking is not about thinking more;
it's about thinking better. In a world filled with noise,
it is the silence of a thoughtful mind that finds clarity."*
– Vandana

In today's fast-paced world, we are often overwhelmed with information, constantly bombarded by opinions, and urged to make decisions quickly. It is easy to fall into the trap of making hasty judgements or simply following the crowd. However, critical thinking—the ability to analyse information objectively, assess arguments, and evaluate solutions—remains one of the most essential skills for success in life and business. In this chapter, we will explore how developing critical thinking as a lifelong habit can transform the way we approach problems, make decisions, and interact with the world around us.

Why Critical Thinking Matters

Critical thinking is the cornerstone of good decision-making. It is the process of objectively evaluating information, identifying biases, recognising assumptions, and using logic to draw conclusions. As society becomes more complex and interconnected, the need for critical thinking has never been more urgent. Whether we are navigating personal relationships, tackling professional challenges, or even deciding on what to believe, critical thinking enables us to make informed, practical decisions.

Without it, we risk falling prey to misconceptions, relying on faulty logic, or making decisions based on incomplete or biased information. In contrast, developing strong analytical skills allows us to assess situations from multiple angles, challenge our assumptions, and seek solutions that are grounded in reality.

Developing Analytical Skills for Everyday Situations

Critical thinking is not reserved for solving complex, high-stakes problems. It is a skill that can be applied to everyday situations, from deciding how to manage our time more effectively to determining the best course of action in an interpersonal conflict. By honing our analytical skills, we become better equipped to navigate the complexities of daily life with clarity and confidence.

1. Question Assumptions:

At the heart of critical thinking is the ability to question assumptions. We all make assumptions based on past experiences, cultural influences, or societal norms. However, not all assumptions are accurate, and they can sometimes lead us astray. By questioning assumptions, we can uncover hidden biases and open ourselves up to new possibilities.

Story: Elon Musk and Challenging Assumptions

Elon Musk, the entrepreneur behind Tesla and SpaceX, is known for his ability to question conventional assumptions. When Musk decided to build reusable rockets for space travel, the prevailing assumption in the aerospace industry was that rockets had to be single-use, as they were too expensive to recycle. Rather than accepting this as a given, Musk questioned it and pursued a different approach. The result? SpaceX successfully developed reusable rockets, significantly reducing the cost of space travel.

Lesson:

By challenging assumptions, we can break free from conventional thinking and open the door to innovative solutions.

2. Break Down Problems into Manageable Parts:

Critical thinking also involves breaking down complex problems into smaller, more manageable components. This process allows us to better understand the issue at hand, identify key variables, and determine a step-by-step approach to solving it.

Story: The Founder of Zappos and Simplifying a Business Model

Tony Hsieh, the founder of Zappos, applied critical thinking when he approached the idea of selling shoes online. At the time, many people doubted that customers would buy shoes without trying them on first. Hsieh broke down the problem: what were the core elements that would convince customers to make a purchase? By offering free returns, a hassle-free return policy, and excellent customer service, Zappos simplified the shoe-buying process and built a thriving online business.

Lesson:

By breaking down complex challenges into smaller, manageable parts, we can find practical solutions that address the core issues.

3. Use Evidence and Logic:

Critical thinking requires us to rely on evidence and logic rather than intuition or emotion. In everyday decision-making, it can be tempting to go with our gut feeling, but a logical, evidence-based approach is often more reliable. Look for data, facts, and research to support your decisions.

Story: Ratan Tata and the Nano Car

Ratan Tata, the chairman of Tata Group, demonstrated the power of evidence-based critical thinking when he set out to create the world's cheapest car, the Tata Nano. While many in the automotive industry doubted the feasibility of such a car, Tata analysed the market, understood the needs of the lower-income population, and gathered data to create a solution. The result was a car priced at just $2,000, making it affordable for millions of people in India.

Lesson:

Critical thinking involves gathering evidence, using logic, and applying data to make informed decisions.

Avoiding Overthinking and Finding Practical Solutions

While critical thinking is an invaluable skill, it is important to avoid overthinking. Overthinking occurs when we get caught up in an endless loop of possibilities, anxieties, and uncertainties, preventing us from taking action. Critical thinking, when done right, should lead to practical, grounded decisions, not paralysing indecision.

1. Identify the Root Cause of the Problem:

Overthinking often arises when we focus too much on surface-level symptoms instead of the root cause. By identifying the core issue, we can avoid getting lost in irrelevant details and come up with a practical solution.

Story: Warren Buffet's Simple Approach to Investing

Warren Buffet, one of the most successful investors of all time, is known for his simple, common-sense approach to investing. He focuses on identifying the core value of a company and avoids getting distracted by short-term fluctuations in the stock market. Buffet's critical thinking is rooted in identifying the fundamental drivers of value rather than over-complicating things with extraneous information.

Lesson:

By focusing on the root cause of a problem, we can simplify our thinking and avoid over-complicating solutions.

2. Embrace Decision-Making Frameworks:

Overthinking often occurs when we are unsure how to approach a decision. One way to combat this is by using decision-making frameworks. These frameworks provide a structured approach to evaluating options and making decisions. Common frameworks include cost-benefit analysis, pros and cons lists, and SWOT analysis.

Story: Indra Nooyi and Strategic Decision-Making

Indra Nooyi, the former CEO of PepsiCo, is known for her strategic decision-making. She embraced frameworks such as the Balanced Scorecard to guide her leadership decisions, ensuring that PepsiCo's growth was both sustainable and profitable. Nooyi's disciplined approach to decision-making allowed her to navigate complex business challenges without falling into the trap of overthinking.

Lesson:

By using decision-making frameworks, we can reduce the risk of overthinking and make more informed, efficient choices.

3. Trust Your Judgement and Act Quickly:

Another key to avoiding overthinking is learning to trust your judgement and make decisions quickly. While it's important to think critically, there comes a point when prolonged deliberation becomes counterproductive. Trusting your intuition and taking action can often lead to better outcomes than endlessly analysing possibilities.

Story: Sara Blakely and the Leap of Faith

Sara Blakely, the founder of Spanx, demonstrated the power of trusting one's judgement when she decided to start her shapewear company. With no background in fashion or retail, Blakely trusted her instincts and took a leap of faith. She quickly acted on her idea, iterating her product based on customer feedback, rather than overthinking her way to perfection. Today, Spanx is a billion-dollar business.

Lesson:

At some point, overthinking must give way to action. Trusting your judgement and moving forward with confidence is often the best course of action.

Developing Critical Thinking as a Lifelong Habit

Critical thinking is not something we can master overnight—it is a lifelong habit that requires consistent effort. However, with practice, anyone can develop and strengthen their analytical abilities. Here are some strategies for cultivating critical thinking as a lifelong habit:

1. Make Reflection a Routine:

Take time regularly to reflect on your experiences, decisions, and thought processes. Ask yourself questions like: *What assumptions did I make? What could I have done differently? What was the outcome of my decision?* Reflection helps you improve your thinking over time and encourages continuous learning.

2. Challenge Yourself to Think in Different Ways:

Intentionally put yourself in situations that require you to think differently. This might mean engaging with people who have different perspectives, learning about topics outside your expertise, or tackling unfamiliar problems. The more you stretch your thinking, the more flexible and adaptable your critical thinking skills become.

3. Stay Curious:

Curiosity is the foundation of critical thinking. Never stop asking questions and seeking answers. Whether you are learning about a new field, exploring a different culture, or diving deeper into a familiar subject, curiosity drives you to think critically and explore new possibilities.

Conclusion

Critical thinking is a lifelong habit that can be developed through conscious effort, practice, and reflection. By questioning assumptions, breaking down problems, using evidence and logic, and avoiding overthinking, we can become more effective decision-makers in all areas of our lives. In a world filled with distractions and noise, critical thinking enables us to focus on what truly matters, make informed choices, and navigate complex challenges with confidence.

"Critical thinking is the habit of questioning everything and thinking for yourself—it's the key to a more thoughtful, intentional, and successful life."
— Vandana

Reflection Questions

1. How can you practice critical thinking in your daily life, starting with small decisions?

2. What assumptions have you made recently that might need to be re-evaluated?

3. How can you embrace decision-making frameworks to simplify your choices?

Plan of Action

- Start by reflecting on one major decision you made recently. Break it down to identify where critical thinking could have played a role.

- Identify one decision-making framework and apply it to a current problem you are facing.

- Set aside time each week to engage in a new learning experience that challenges your thinking.

Chapter 13

Awareness and Adaptability

> *"The measure of intelligence is the ability to change."*
> *— Albert Einstein*

In today's rapidly evolving world, change is the only constant. Whether in our personal lives or professional careers, the pace of transformation is accelerating, often bringing challenges that we must navigate with a mix of skill, patience, and, most importantly, awareness. At the core of navigating this change successfully lies one of the most essential qualities: adaptability. Adaptability, fuelled by awareness, allows individuals to stay relevant, solve problems effectively, and seize opportunities that others might miss. In this chapter, we will explore the concept of awareness and adaptability—what they mean, why they are crucial for success, and how we can cultivate these qualities in our own lives.

The Power of Awareness

Awareness is the foundation upon which adaptability is built. It is the ability to perceive and understand what is happening around us, without being clouded by distractions, assumptions, or biases. It allows us to stay present in the moment, to truly grasp the dynamics of any situation, and to understand ourselves, our emotions, and the world with clarity. Without awareness, we may miss opportunities, fail to recognise potential threats, or react impulsively rather than thoughtfully.

Staying Present in the Moment

At its core, awareness is about staying present—being fully engaged with the here and now. In a world filled with distractions, it is easy to drift through life on autopilot, focusing on tasks and goals without truly engaging with our environment or the people around us. Yet, mindfulness—the practice of staying present—allows us to be more aware of what's happening in real time, which enables us to respond appropriately rather than react impulsively.

Story: Steve Jobs and His Zen Influence

Steve Jobs, the co-founder of Apple, was famously influenced by Zen Buddhism, which emphasises mindfulness and living in the present moment. Jobs was known for his deep focus, spending hours in reflection and allowing his intuition to guide his decisions. His awareness of design, user experience, and the future of technology led Apple to create products that transformed entire industries. Jobs' ability to stay present and focused on the task at hand, while being open to new ideas and changes, played a significant role in his success.

Lesson:

Being fully present allows us to make better decisions and understand our environment more clearly, which in turn leads to more effective responses to change.

Adaptability: Responding to Change

Adaptability is the ability to adjust to new conditions and embrace change rather than resist it. In the business world, those who fail to adapt often find themselves left behind as their industries evolve. On the other hand, individuals who can quickly assess a new situation, understand the underlying challenges, and modify their strategies accordingly tend to thrive. Adaptability requires a combination of emotional intelligence, awareness, and resilience.

The Role of Awareness in Adaptability

Being adaptable is not just about reacting to changes—it's about being prepared for them. Awareness helps us to anticipate change before it arrives, to notice the subtle shifts in trends, and to understand the dynamics that shape our decisions. By cultivating awareness, we position ourselves to respond with flexibility, rather than being blindsided by new developments.

Story: Reed Hastings and Netflix's Transformation

Reed Hastings, the co-founder of Netflix, is a prime example of someone who demonstrated adaptability and awareness. In the early 2000s, Netflix was a DVD rental service, but Hastings saw the emerging trend of streaming and made the bold decision to shift the business model. While many others were hesitant to disrupt their existing business, Hastings foresaw the inevitable decline of physical rentals and made a strategic pivot. His ability to anticipate the changing entertainment landscape and adapt Netflix's offerings was a key reason behind the company's massive success.

Lesson:

Being aware of external trends and shifts allows us to take proactive steps toward adapting, instead of merely reacting when change occurs.

Building Awareness: Practical Steps

While some people seem to have a natural ability to stay aware and adaptable, these qualities can be developed with practice. Building awareness requires discipline, focus, and a willingness to reflect on ourselves and our environment. Below are some practical steps to help cultivate awareness:

1. Practice Mindfulness:

Mindfulness is the practice of paying attention to the present moment without judgement. It is about noticing the details in our surroundings, our thoughts, and our feelings. By engaging in mindfulness exercises such as meditation, deep breathing, or even mindful walking, we can improve our ability to stay present and aware.

Story: Arianna Huffington and the Importance of Sleep

Arianna Huffington, the co-founder of The Huffington Post, emphasises the importance of mindfulness in maintaining awareness. After collapsing from exhaustion due to poor sleep habits, she became an advocate for sleep and mindfulness as essential components of success. Huffington's awareness of the detrimental effects of burnout led her to launch Thrive Global, a company that promotes well-being and mindfulness as key to professional and personal success.

Lesson:

Mindfulness not only improves awareness but also helps in reducing stress, leading to better decision-making and adaptability in all areas of life.

2. Engage in Active Listening:

To be truly aware, we must listen actively—not just to others, but also to ourselves. Active listening involves focusing entirely on the speaker, understanding their message, responding thoughtfully, and remembering key details. This practice helps us stay attuned to others' needs, opinions, and emotions, which is essential in both personal and professional relationships.

Story: Oprah Winfrey's Empathy and Active Listening

Oprah Winfrey is known for her exceptional ability to listen deeply and with empathy. Whether interviewing world leaders, authors, or everyday people, Oprah's awareness and attentiveness allow her to connect with her guests on a profound level. Her active listening skills have helped her create meaningful conversations that resonate with millions, while also enabling her to adapt to diverse situations and topics.

Lesson:

Active listening is a key practice that enhances our awareness of others' perspectives and allows us to engage with the world in a more thoughtful, responsive way.

3. Reflect on Your Emotions and Reactions:

Awareness is not just about observing the external world; it's also about being attuned to our internal reactions. Our emotions can shape our decisions and influence our ability to adapt to new situations. By reflecting on our emotions and understanding what triggers them, we can respond more effectively and avoid impulsive decisions.

Story: Barack Obama and Emotional Control

Former President Barack Obama is known for his calm and measured demeanour, even in high-pressure situations. Obama's ability to maintain awareness of his emotions, particularly in the face of stress and adversity, allowed him to adapt to the constantly changing demands of the presidency. His emotional intelligence and self-awareness were crucial to his success in making tough decisions.

Lesson:

By reflecting on our emotions, we gain a deeper understanding of ourselves and our reactions, which helps us adapt in challenging situations.

Learning from Successful Individuals Who Embody Awareness

Throughout history, many successful individuals have embodied the qualities of awareness and adaptability. Their ability to stay present and responsive to change has been key to their success. Below are a few notable examples of individuals who have excelled in this area:

1. Richard Branson and his Adaptability in Business:

Richard Branson, the founder of the Virgin Group, is known for his fearless adaptability. Over the years, Branson has successfully launched and managed ventures in diverse industries, from music to airlines to space travel. His ability to adapt to new markets, industries, and business models has been crucial to his success. Branson's awareness of emerging trends, his willingness to take risks, and his ability to pivot when necessary have enabled him to stay ahead of the curve.

Lesson:

Branson's ability to read the market and adjust his strategy accordingly exemplifies the power of adaptability and awareness in business.

2. Maya Angelou and Her Emotional Awareness:

Maya Angelou, the renowned author and poet, demonstrated incredible emotional awareness throughout her life. She was keenly aware of the emotional landscapes of the people around her, and her works often focused on themes of resilience, empathy, and emotional intelligence. Angelou's ability to understand her own emotions and those of others allowed her to connect deeply with people and make a lasting impact through her writing and speaking.

Lesson:

Emotional awareness not only fosters empathy but also allows us to respond to others with greater sensitivity and understanding, which is essential in navigating life's challenges.

3. Jeff Bezos and Long-Term Awareness:

Jeff Bezos, the founder of Amazon, is known for his forward-thinking vision and adaptability. His awareness of the growing importance of e-commerce in the late 1990s led him to create Amazon, initially as an online bookstore. Over the years, Bezos adapted the business model to include everything from cloud computing to entertainment, all while remaining aware of the technological trends shaping the future. His ability to anticipate long-term changes in consumer behaviour and technology has made Amazon a global powerhouse.

Lesson:

Bezos' success is rooted in his awareness of emerging trends and his ability to adapt his business strategy over time.

Conclusion

Awareness and adaptability are not just skills—they are mindsets that shape how we approach the world. By staying present, attuned to our surroundings, and responsive to change, we position ourselves to thrive in an ever-evolving landscape. Successful individuals, from entrepreneurs like Steve Jobs and Richard Branson to thought leaders like Maya Angelou, all embody the principles of awareness and adaptability. These qualities allow them to make informed decisions, navigate challenges, and continuously grow, both personally and professionally.

As we move forward in our own lives, it is essential to cultivate these traits. Awareness, through practices like mindfulness and active listening, helps us stay grounded in the present, while adaptability enables us to respond effectively to new circumstances. Together, they form a powerful foundation for navigating the complexities of life and seizing opportunities in a world of constant change.

True adaptability is rooted in the depth of awareness—when we are present and attuned to our surroundings, we become equipped to respond to change, not just react to it."
– *Vandana*

Introspective Questions

1. What are some areas in your life where you need to become more aware of your surroundings, emotions, and decisions?

2. How can you increase your adaptability in the face of personal or professional changes?

3. Who in your life exemplifies awareness and adaptability, and what lessons can you learn from them?

Plan of Action

- Practice mindfulness daily, even for just 5 minutes, to increase your present-moment awareness.

- Engage in active listening during your next conversation, focusing fully on understanding the speaker.

- Reflect on a recent change you experienced and assess how adaptable you were to it. What could you have done differently?

Chapter 14

The Intersection of Common-Sense and Technology

*"Technology is a tool, not the answer.
The true power lies in how we apply it with
wisdom and common-sense."*
– Ankur

Introduction

We live in an age where technology's influence is inescapable. Every industry, every facet of life is touched by innovation—from artificial intelligence (AI) to machine learning (ML), automation, and the ever-expanding digital landscape. While these technologies bring immense potential to drive change, they also present new challenges. How do we ensure that our innate human wisdom—our common-sense—remains central in an increasingly tech-dependent world? How do we use technology without becoming slaves to it, and how do we balance the reliance on advanced systems with the simplicity and practicality of common-sense?

In this chapter, we will explore how common-sense remains a vital skill in navigating the digital age. We will discuss how successful people, both globally and in India, have applied common-sense to make sound decisions in their use of technology. Through practical examples and real-world stories, we'll highlight the importance of balancing technological reliance with human judgement, ensuring that innovation doesn't overshadow reason. Finally, we'll dive into how AI and ML, though powerful, can be complemented by common-sense to make truly impactful decisions.

Using Common-Sense to Navigate the Digital Age

In today's world, we are surrounded by information and innovation. We can access anything and everything at the touch of a button—news, advice, entertainment, even relationships. However, with this access comes complexity. There is often too much data, too many choices, and not enough clear guidance on how to navigate them. This is where common-sense becomes crucial.

The Rise of Social Media: A Double-Edged Sword

One of the most poignant examples of how common-sense intersects with technology is seen in the rise of social media. Platforms like Facebook, Twitter, Instagram, and TikTok have revolutionised how we connect with others. These platforms provide a space for expression, education, and entertainment. However, they also amplify misinformation, create echo chambers, and contribute to the spread of fake news.

A prime example of someone using common-sense to navigate this world is **Sundar Pichai**, the CEO of Google. Pichai has consistently emphasised the importance of responsible technology use. When faced with the rapid spread of misinformation during critical global events (like elections or the pandemic), Pichai and his team at Google applied common-sense in regulating how information is shared on their platforms. Instead of simply relying on algorithms, Pichai made the decision to balance tech-driven solutions with human oversight and judgement.

For instance, Google's efforts to tackle misinformation regarding COVID-19 involved using AI to identify harmful content but also applying human fact-checking systems to ensure that the information being shared was accurate and responsible. This combination of tech and common-sense allowed Google to maintain credibility and trust, while also keeping the user experience transparent and humane.

The Overload of Data: Cutting Through the Noise

In the digital age, information overload is a constant. With so much data available, how do we ensure that we are focusing on what truly matters? Common-sense tells us to filter the noise, ignore the distractions, and focus on what's relevant.

A perfect example of this comes from **Tim Cook**, the CEO of Apple. In his approach to leadership, Cook has always been focused on simplicity—both in design and in the way Apple engages with technology. One of Cook's guiding principles was to simplify the user experience. For example, when Apple introduced the iPhone, the idea was to make the most powerful device on the market easy to use, with intuitive features that anyone could understand.

Rather than overwhelming users with unnecessary features, Cook used common-sense to focus on the essentials. This not only helped Apple revolutionise the smartphone industry but also showcased how, in a world full of endless data and options, focusing on simplicity and clarity can lead to extraordinary success.

Balancing Tech Reliance with Human Judgement

While technology offers incredible opportunities, it also raises important questions about human judgement. Can we trust machines to make critical decisions for us? Should we allow AI to control aspects of our lives, or is there a place for human intuition and insight in decision-making?

The Role of Human Intuition in Decision-Making

Indra Nooyi, the former CEO of PepsiCo, is a shining example of how human judgement and intuition can complement technology in a business context. Nooyi, a successful leader in a data-driven world, always believed in the power of human insight. While she was a firm believer in leveraging data to make business decisions, she never allowed the numbers to dictate her every move.

She once remarked, "Data is important, but it can never replace the human element." During her tenure at PepsiCo, Nooyi was known for making bold decisions based on a combination of hard data and her deep understanding of human behaviour. For instance, when PepsiCo decided to expand into healthier food options, it wasn't just the market data that influenced the decision. Nooyi used her common-sense and intuition to understand the changing consumer trends towards health-conscious living.

By blending technology and human judgement, Nooyi transformed PepsiCo into a company that could stay ahead of trends while also focusing on the needs and desires of its customers. This balance of data and intuition is a powerful demonstration of how common-sense plays a central role in making decisions in the tech-driven world.

Managing Tech-Driven Change: Lessons from India

In India, the application of common-sense in technology is just as important. **Ratan Tata**, the former chairman of Tata Group, exemplifies the application of common-sense when embracing technology. While Tata Group is a conglomerate with operations in various sectors, Ratan Tata's strategic decisions were never solely guided by trends or market hype. Instead, he combined technology with practical judgement, ensuring that his companies focused on long-term goals.

One of Tata's most famous decisions was to acquire **Jaguar Land Rover (JLR)** in 2008, which was initially seen as a risky move. However, Tata's decision was rooted in common-sense. Rather than just relying on financial analysis, he considered the potential for technological synergies, innovation, and future growth. Tata Group integrated advanced technologies into JLR's manufacturing processes, while maintaining the legacy and ethos of the brand. Through his balanced approach, Tata showed that, even in a world driven by technological change, common-sense remains the key to success.

AI/ML and Common-Sense

As artificial intelligence and machine learning continue to grow, we face new challenges in ensuring that these technologies are used responsibly and wisely. AI and ML offer immense potential to automate decision-making, solve complex problems, and predict future trends. But do they always lead to the best outcomes? Is human judgement still required in a world where machines can process data more quickly and accurately than any human?

AI and Human Judgement: A Partnership, Not a Replacement

Take the example of **Satya Nadella**, the CEO of Microsoft. Nadella has been a proponent of AI and machine learning, but he emphasises that these technologies should augment human capabilities, not replace them. Under his leadership, Microsoft's AI strategy focused on ethical guidelines for AI development and usage. Nadella is one of the key figures who consistently advocates for the partnership between human wisdom and machine intelligence.

For instance, when Microsoft developed its AI for healthcare, the company ensured that doctors and healthcare providers remained in control of the final decision-making process. Rather than allowing AI to take over medical diagnoses entirely, the system was designed to assist professionals in making more informed decisions. Nadella's approach exemplifies how common-sense in technology means recognising the boundaries of AI and understanding that it should support human judgement, not replace it.

In India, **Nandan Nilekani**, the co-founder of Infosys and the architect of Aadhaar, India's biometric identification system, has also demonstrated how technology can be used in conjunction with common-sense. When designing Aadhaar, Nilekani ensured that the technology would be used to enhance the delivery of government services without compromising privacy or security. His approach exemplifies the intersection of common-sense and technology—ensuring that while AI and automation make processes more efficient, human values and ethical considerations remain central.

> *"Technology should serve humanity, not replace it.
> Common-sense will always be the compass that guides us,
> even in the most advanced digital age."*
> *— Vandana*

Practical Tips for Navigating the Intersection of Common-Sense and Technology

1. **Don't Blindly Follow Trends**: Technology evolves quickly, but not every trend will be suitable for your situation. Use common-sense to evaluate whether a new technology aligns with your values and objectives.

2. **Integrate Human Judgement with Tech Tools**: Ensure that every technology you use has a layer of human oversight. Whether it's AI, automation, or data analytics, remember that human intuition, empathy, and ethical judgement are irreplaceable.

3. **Focus on What Adds Value**: Avoid the temptation to adopt every new tech solution. Focus on the ones that truly add value to your life or business. Sometimes the simplest solution is the most effective.

4. **Regularly Reassess Your Tech Use**: In a rapidly changing world, it's essential to periodically assess your use of technology. Ask yourself whether it is still serving your needs, and adjust accordingly.

Reflection Questions

1. How often do you rely on technology to make decisions, and how do you ensure that your judgement isn't clouded by it?

2. In what areas of your life or business could you apply more common-sense when using technology?

3. How can you integrate human intuition with AI and automation in your work or personal life?

Plan of Action

1. **Conduct a Technology Audit**: Take a moment to assess all the technologies you currently rely on. Are they helping you make better decisions, or are they complicating things? Eliminate any unnecessary or redundant tools.

2. **Set Boundaries with Tech**: Decide on areas where you can consciously limit your tech usage. Set time blocks for deep, focused work without tech interruptions.

3. **Leverage AI for Support, Not Control**: If you are in a field that uses AI or ML, make sure to use these tools to enhance your judgement, not replace it. Keep humans in the loop, especially when it comes to ethical decisions.

> *"Technology is powerful, but it's our common-sense that makes it truly transformative. It's not the tool, but how we use it that determines its value."*
> *— Vandana*

This chapter invites you to reflect on the importance of common-sense in a technology-driven world. Technology will continue to evolve, but by anchoring ourselves in common-sense, we can navigate the complexities of the digital age with wisdom, clarity, and purpose.

Chapter 15

Common-Sense and Leadership

*"True leadership is not about being in charge.
It's about taking care of those in your charge, and doing
so with practical wisdom."*
– Ankur

Leadership is often seen as a complex, multi-faceted role. Leaders are expected to have vision, charisma, and the ability to inspire others. However, one quality that is frequently overlooked but critical to effective leadership is **common-sense**. Leaders who possess practical wisdom are able to cut through complexity, make sound decisions in uncertain times, and guide their teams with clarity and empathy. In this chapter, we will explore how common-sense plays a central role in leadership, not as a static skill, but as a dynamic and powerful tool for guiding teams, organisations, and even entire nations.

Through stories of influential leaders from various walks of life, both globally and in India, we will understand how common-sense can shape decisions that foster trust, drive success, and inspire those who follow. By examining the leadership styles of well-known figures, we can gain valuable insights into how to cultivate common-sense in leadership roles.

How Leaders Use Practical Wisdom to Inspire and Guide

The role of a leader extends far beyond making decisions. It involves guiding people, creating a shared vision, and ensuring that goals are achieved. The foundation of good leadership is rooted in sound judgement, the ability to think clearly in the face of adversity, and a deep understanding of what is best for the team or organisation. In all of these aspects, common-sense plays a crucial role.

Clarity in Decision-Making

In times of crisis, when the path forward seems unclear, it is the leader who steps forward with calm and clarity. Practical wisdom, or common-sense, allows leaders to make the right decisions based on what is immediately needed, rather than being swayed by external pressures or emotional responses.

Warren Buffet, one of the world's most successful investors, exemplifies this in his leadership style. Buffet's common-sense approach to investing and leadership has been a guiding force for both his company, Berkshire Hathaway, and for the many people who look to him for wisdom. Buffet's ability to see the bigger picture, make long-term decisions, and ignore the noise in the market has been a hallmark of his leadership.

Buffet famously advocates for investing in what you understand, an application of common-sense in a world filled with speculative opportunities. His principle of buying companies with strong fundamentals and holding them for the long-term has proved successful, even when markets become turbulent. In his words, "The stock market is a device for transferring money from the impatient to the patient." Buffet's leadership is grounded in practicality—

making decisions based on knowledge, patience, and common-sense, rather than chasing trends or short-term gains.

Empathy and Listening

A leader's ability to listen to others is one of the most important ways common-sense is applied. Many leaders make the mistake of assuming they have all the answers, but the most successful ones recognise that they don't. Instead, they prioritise listening, understanding the needs of their teams, and making decisions that are in the best interest of everyone.

Take **Satya Nadella**, the CEO of Microsoft, as an example. Nadella is known for his leadership style that emphasises empathy and emotional intelligence. When Nadella took over as CEO of Microsoft, he was faced with the challenge of reviving a company that had stagnated under previous leadership. He recognised that the culture at Microsoft needed a major shift to be more collaborative and inclusive. Nadella applied common-sense by focusing on listening to employees, understanding their concerns, and creating a culture of trust.

One of his first actions was to shift Microsoft's focus from an internally competitive culture to one of collaboration. Nadella emphasised the importance of empathy within the workplace and led by example, fostering open communication and giving his team a sense of ownership. His pragmatic approach, grounded in listening and empathy, has been instrumental in turning around Microsoft's culture and performance.

Guiding Through Change

Leaders are often tasked with leading organisations through times of great change. This can include restructuring, technological disruption, or navigating a crisis. The ability to stay grounded and make decisions based on common-sense is critical during such transitions.

Indra Nooyi, the former CEO of PepsiCo, demonstrated this brilliantly. During her tenure, Nooyi navigated PepsiCo through a period of dramatic change. She successfully led the company to expand its portfolio beyond just soda, focusing on healthier food and beverage options in response to growing consumer demands.

Nooyi's decision to focus on health-conscious products was a practical one, driven by her common-sense understanding of market trends and consumer behaviour. Instead of simply following the competition or pursuing short-term profits, Nooyi steered PepsiCo towards a sustainable future. She once said, "The toughest thing in leadership is to do the right thing when it's not popular." Her practical, no-nonsense approach to leadership, always grounded in real-world considerations, shows how common-sense can be an invaluable tool for navigating complex challenges.

Stories of Influential Leaders Who Champion Common-Sense

Let's now take a closer look at several influential leaders—global and Indian—who embody the essence of common-sense in their leadership.

Nelson Mandela: Leading with Purpose and Simplicity

Nelson Mandela, the former President of South Africa and anti-apartheid revolutionary, is another leader who demonstrated the power of common-sense in leadership. Mandela's ability to unite a divided nation through his simple yet profound sense of justice and fairness is legendary. After spending 27 years in prison, Mandela could have easily chosen to lead with anger and vengeance, but he chose common-sense over retribution.

Mandela's leadership was based on understanding the complexities of human nature, and he used practical wisdom to foster peace and reconciliation in South Africa. His famous quote, "I am not a saint, unless you think of a saint as a sinner who keeps on trying," reflects his grounded approach. Rather than letting the weight of history or the bitterness of the past cloud his judgement, Mandela applied common-sense by focusing on what would benefit the future of his nation, not what would perpetuate division.

Mandela's practical wisdom ensured that his leadership was focused on healing and uniting South Africa, guiding the country through one of its most critical transitions without allowing ideology or emotion to derail progress.

Ratan Tata: Leading with Integrity and Pragmatism

In India, **Ratan Tata** is a prime example of a leader who used common-sense to guide his organisation to success. Tata's leadership style is marked by a deep sense of integrity and a focus on long-term growth, rather than short-term wins. His decision to acquire **Jaguar Land Rover** in 2008, amidst the global financial crisis, is an example of his practical wisdom. While many saw the acquisition as a risky move, Tata recognised the strategic value it would bring to the Tata Group and its global presence.

Tata's leadership was also marked by his personal commitment to social responsibility, with initiatives like the Tata Trusts, which focus on improving healthcare, education, and rural development in India. His ability to balance business interests with social causes shows how common-sense, combined with a strong moral compass, can lead to sustainable and meaningful success.

Sundar Pichai: Navigating Innovation with Clear Vision

Another modern example of leadership grounded in common-sense is **Sundar Pichai**, the CEO of Google and its parent company, Alphabet. Pichai's leadership has been shaped by his ability to simplify complex challenges and prioritise long-term goals. As a leader of one of the world's largest tech companies, Pichai has been at the forefront of navigating both technological innovations and ethical dilemmas.

In 2015, under Pichai's leadership, Google restructured itself to form Alphabet, a more diversified holding company. This was a move rooted in common-sense—allowing Google's core business to focus on its search engine and advertising platforms, while its other ventures, like Waymo (self-driving cars) and Verily (life sciences), could operate with more autonomy. Pichai's pragmatic decision-making, often driven by his clear vision and practical insight, has been instrumental in keeping Google at the forefront of the tech world.

Practical Tips for Developing Common-Sense in Leadership

1. **Keep It Simple**: Leaders should avoid over-complicating decisions. Simplicity and clarity often lead to the best outcomes. Focus on the core issues and make decisions based on common-sense, rather than trying to please everyone or follow complex trends.

2. **Listen More Than You Speak**: Leadership is about understanding the needs of others. Prioritise listening to your team members and considering their perspectives before making decisions.

3. **Stay Grounded in Reality**: Avoid being swayed by idealism or abstract theories. Ground your decisions in real-world data, practical considerations, and your own experiences.

4. **Be Decisive, Not Impulsive**: Common-sense leaders are decisive, but they don't make rash decisions. Weigh the options, consider the long-term implications, and then make a decision.

Reflection Questions

1. How can you incorporate more common-sense into your leadership style? What decisions can you make today that would reflect this?

2. Who are some leaders you admire for their common-sense approach, and what can you learn from their methods?

3. When faced with difficult choices, how do you ensure that you stay grounded and make practical decisions?

Plan of Action

1. **Evaluate Your Leadership Approach**: Reflect on your current leadership style. Are you using common-sense to guide your decisions? What changes can you make to ensure your leadership is grounded in practicality?

2. **Seek Feedback**: Ask for feedback from your team. Are they following your lead with clarity and confidence? What practical suggestions can they offer to improve your leadership?

3. **Make Simpler Decisions**: Start by simplifying one area of your leadership. Maybe it's how you communicate, how you delegate, or how you approach problem-solving. Focus on the essentials, and use your common-sense to navigate the complexity.

> *"Leadership is about knowing when to lead with your mind and when to lead with your heart. And above all, it's about leading with common-sense."*
> *– Vandana*

Additional Leadership Stories from New-Age Startups and Unicorns

In today's fast-paced and ever-evolving business environment, the leaders of startups and unicorns must navigate complex challenges, balancing rapid growth, innovation, and sustainability. What makes them successful is often their ability to apply common-sense in a rapidly changing world. Here are 3 such stories from the leaders of new-age startups and unicorns who have used practical wisdom to shape their organisations.

1. Byju Raveendran: Leading Education with a Vision

Byju Raveendran, the co-founder and CEO of **BYJU'S**, India's leading edtech unicorn, is a prime example of a leader who combines common-sense with innovation. Byju's journey from a small startup to a global edtech giant is a testament to the power of simplicity, practical decision-making, and understanding what customers truly need.

Byju Raveendran's path to success was grounded in understanding one simple yet profound truth: education should be engaging and accessible. Instead of over-complicating the process of learning, he focused on making it interactive and fun. He saw that traditional methods of learning weren't resonating with students, especially in a digital age, so he developed an approach that combined visual learning with technology.

Byju's common-sense approach was seen during the early stages of BYJU'S when Raveendran pivoted from offline to online education. While many in the education sector were unsure about the potential of online learning, Byju's practical foresight allowed him to identify the market demand early on. During the pandemic, when physical classrooms were closed, BYJU'S emerged as one of the most trusted platforms for learning, further solidifying Raveendran's decision to prioritise technology-driven, user-centric learning.

Raveendran's approach to leadership is pragmatic: he focuses on empowering his employees, creating a culture of innovation, and constantly adapting to changing needs. His decisions are informed by deep market insights and a focus on creating value, rather than just chasing revenue growth.

Key Takeaway: Byju's leadership is built on the common-sense principle that education must be simple, effective, and engaging. His ability to pivot at the right time and make data-driven decisions enabled BYJU'S to scale successfully.

2. Kunal Shah: Building a Consumer-Centric Business with Common-Sense

Kunal Shah, the founder and CEO of **CRED**, a fintech unicorn that has disrupted India's credit card payments and rewards space, exemplifies how practical wisdom can be the driving force behind a startup's success. Kunal's approach to leadership is often centred around deeply understanding consumer psychology and providing simple, intuitive solutions to complex financial problems.

CRED's core offering—rewarding users for paying their credit card bills—was a brilliant example of common-sense. While the fintech world was focusing on more complex financial solutions like lending and investment, Shah saw an untapped market in incentivising good financial behaviour. He identified that credit card users were often penalised for late payments but were not rewarded for responsible behaviour. By offering rewards for timely payments, Shah created a value proposition that was both simple and effective.

Kunal Shah's leadership style is rooted in making decisions based on user behaviour, real-time feedback, and a clear understanding of market needs. One of his most important leadership strategies is to constantly engage with customers and get feedback directly from them, ensuring that the company's growth is driven by actual demand. His common-sense approach to solving real-world problems, without over-complicating the solutions, has helped CRED grow exponentially in a short amount of time.

Shah also believes in the importance of creating a strong company culture, one that encourages collaboration, open communication, and risk-taking. His common-sense leadership doesn't just focus on growth but also on creating long-term, sustainable relationships with customers and employees alike.

Key Takeaway: Kunal Shah's leadership is a clear example of how understanding consumer behaviour and simplifying complex financial challenges with practical solutions can lead to startup success. His ability to listen to users and create an engaging, rewarding platform speaks to the power of common-sense in leadership.

3. Deepinder Goyal: Innovating with Common-Sense at Zomato

Deepinder Goyal, the co-founder and CEO of **Zomato**, one of India's leading food delivery and restaurant discovery platforms, has demonstrated practical wisdom in building a company that serves millions of users while constantly evolving with the needs of the market. Goyal's leadership in growing Zomato from a small startup to a global unicorn is a testament to the power of simplicity and common-sense in navigating the challenges of entrepreneurship.

Zomato's journey was built on common-sense solutions to real-world problems. Goyal initially launched the company as **Foodiebay**, an online restaurant guide. However, after understanding that users needed more than just restaurant information, he pivoted to a full-fledged food delivery platform. This shift, while not revolutionary, was a pragmatic decision that was guided by a clear understanding of consumer demand and behaviour.

During the early days of Zomato, Goyal made the strategic decision to keep things simple—offering essential services such as accurate restaurant reviews and timely delivery. He avoided over-complicating the business model by not introducing unnecessary features and instead focused on building a smooth, customer-centric user experience.

As Zomato grew, Goyal faced the challenge of global expansion. His common-sense approach involved focusing on markets with a similar food delivery culture and launching services in smaller steps to ensure scalability. Zomato's success in international markets like the UAE and Australia was due to Goyal's decision to focus on markets that could benefit from Zomato's unique value proposition.

Through practical, data-driven decision-making, Goyal has steered Zomato through competition, regulatory challenges, and market changes, ensuring that the company remains relevant in the fast-paced food delivery industry. His leadership is marked by a focus on customer satisfaction, data-driven decisions, and a pragmatic approach to market growth.

Key Takeaway: Deepinder Goyal's leadership showcases how common-sense can guide a company through market challenges, customer demands, and international expansion. His focus on simplicity, user experience, and adaptability in leadership has allowed Zomato to grow into a unicorn.

Final Reflections

As we've explored, common-sense is an invaluable asset for leaders across industries and markets. The stories of Byju Raveendran, Kunal Shah, and Deepinder Goyal all illustrate how practical wisdom, grounded in real-world understanding, can propel businesses to great success. These leaders understood the importance of simplicity, customer-centricity, and adaptability, making decisions that were both straightforward and impactful.

Reflection Questions

1. How can you apply the common-sense principles demonstrated by these leaders in your own leadership journey?

2. What simple decisions can you make today to improve your leadership effectiveness?

3. How do you ensure that your leadership is grounded in practicality and real-world understanding, rather than over-complicating things?

Plan of Action

1. **Evaluate and Simplify**: Review your current leadership approach. Are there any areas where you can simplify processes or decision-making to ensure better clarity and effectiveness?

2. **Focus on User-Centric Solutions**: Like Kunal Shah and Byju Raveendran, ensure that your decisions are grounded in the needs and feedback of those you lead, whether they are customers, employees, or stakeholders.

3. **Adapt to Change**: Leaders in today's world must be adaptable. Identify one area where you can lead with more flexibility and responsiveness to change, just like Deepinder Goyal did with Zomato's expansion strategy.

> ***"The best leaders are those who combine
> practicality with vision, and common-sense with
> innovation. Lead with your mind, and your
> heart will follow."***
> **– Vandana**

Additional Leadership Stories from New-Age Startups and Unicorns

The world of startups and unicorns is rapidly evolving, and the leaders who guide these companies through constant changes often rely on a core principle—common-sense. Here are 4 more inspiring stories of leaders from some of the world's most successful startups and unicorns, whose common-sense approach to leadership has made all the difference.

4. Ritesh Agarwal: Building OYO Rooms with Vision and Simplicity

Ritesh Agarwal, the founder and CEO of **OYO Rooms**, one of the world's largest and most successful hotel chains, epitomises the role of practical wisdom in leadership. Agarwal, who started his journey with OYO at the age of 19, is a prime example of how applying common-sense and understanding a real-world problem can lead to exponential growth.

Agarwal was keenly aware of the need for affordable, consistent hotel accommodation in India. With the hospitality industry being fragmented and riddled with inconsistent standards, he saw an opportunity to create a reliable and standardised offering. OYO's rise was based on simplifying the hotel-booking process and providing customers with value-for-money rooms that met a basic standard of quality.

Ritesh's leadership and decision-making have always been rooted in common-sense principles. He prioritised building a scalable business model from the beginning, focusing on creating a network of partner hotels with standardised amenities, without getting bogged down by the complexities of running individual hotel operations. By leveraging technology to optimise operations, manage pricing, and streamline booking systems, he was able to disrupt the hotel industry.

Agarwal also employed a simple strategy to recruit partners and employees. Instead of focusing on hiring large teams, he focused on hiring a small, motivated team that would truly embody the vision and mission of OYO. This allowed OYO to scale rapidly, ultimately transforming the global hotel industry.

Key Takeaway: Ritesh Agarwal's leadership story is an example of how identifying a real-world problem, simplifying it, and applying practical solutions can create a thriving business model. His leadership focused on providing clear value to customers and creating an operational framework that could easily scale.

5. Harshil Mathur & Shashank Kumar: Innovating Finance with Razorpay

Harshil Mathur and **Shashank Kumar**, co-founders of **Razorpay**, a leading fintech unicorn, are reshaping how businesses in India make payments. Razorpay's success story is one of practicality, common-sense, and solving real-world challenges faced by small businesses and startups when it comes to accepting payments.

In India, digital payment solutions were often complicated, unreliable, and costly for small businesses. Harshil and Shashank saw an opportunity to simplify the payment process, making it seamless for merchants to accept payments online without the cumbersome bureaucracy typically associated with banking and payment gateways. Their vision was simple—create a product that would make accepting payments as easy as possible, especially for small and medium-sized enterprises (SMEs).

The co-founders used common-sense to identify that small businesses often struggled with traditional payment systems due to high costs, technical complexities, and a lack of support. They designed Razorpay's platform to be simple, user-friendly, and inclusive, empowering businesses to collect payments easily across different payment channels, including UPI, cards, and wallets.

Through a keen understanding of the payment needs of their customers, Harshil and Shashank built Razorpay into one of India's most successful unicorns. They continuously adapted their services to meet the needs of their customers, such as introducing new products like Razorpay Capital (for providing loans to small businesses) and RazorpayX (a neobank for businesses), without over-complicating their core offering.

Key Takeaway: Harshil and Shashank's leadership at Razorpay demonstrates how understanding your customers' pain points and offering simple, effective solutions can disrupt an industry. Their focus on customer-centric innovation and clear value creation has helped make Razorpay a success.

6. Vijay Shekhar Sharma: The Common-Sense Approach to Digital Payments at Paytm

Vijay Shekhar Sharma, the founder and CEO of **Paytm**, is one of India's most successful entrepreneurs in the fintech space. Paytm's journey from a mobile recharge service to a multi-faceted digital payments and financial services giant is a story rooted in common-sense and adaptability.

Sharma identified an obvious yet largely overlooked problem in India's payments system: the lack of convenient, cashless payment methods for the masses. While digital payments had already gained traction in the Western world, India was still a largely cash-dependent economy. Sharma's insight was simple—build a platform that could integrate seamlessly into users' daily lives, offering everything from mobile recharges to bill payments and eventually, digital wallets and banking services.

Sharma's ability to understand the needs of ordinary people, especially in rural areas, allowed Paytm to cater to a massive market. He saw that while smartphones were becoming increasingly affordable, many people still did not have access to basic banking services. Paytm's mobile wallet became an accessible tool for millions, even in the most remote corners of the country, simply because it addressed a practical need in an easy to use manner.

During the 2016 demonetisation in India, Paytm capitalised on the sudden demand for digital payments. Sharma, using his common-sense leadership, quickly ensured that Paytm remained top-of-mind during this time, further solidifying its place in the market.

Key Takeaway: Vijay Shekhar Sharma's leadership exemplifies how understanding market realities and focusing on simplicity, ease of use, and practicality can lead to business success. His ability to tap into an underserved market, combined with his vision to bring about inclusive growth through digital payments, has made Paytm a household name in India.

7. Falguni Nayar: The Common-Sense Leadership Behind Nykaa's Success

Falguni Nayar, the founder and CEO of **Nykaa**, a leading beauty and wellness e-commerce platform in India, is a great example of how common-sense can be a guiding force in scaling businesses, especially in industries that seem oversaturated or highly competitive.

Nayar's journey began with her realisation that the Indian beauty and cosmetics market lacked a centralised platform offering a wide range of authentic beauty products. At the time, offline retail stores were the primary means of shopping for beauty products, but they were often poorly stocked, with limited choices. Recognising a gap in the market, Nayar launched Nykaa in 2012 with the aim of offering consumers an e-commerce platform that provided quality, authentic products and expert beauty advice, all in one place.

Nayar's leadership is characterised by her ability to use common-sense to make bold decisions. Her pragmatic approach included a unique blend of online and offline strategies. For example, she expanded Nykaa's physical presence by opening flagship stores in major cities, which allowed her to reach a wider audience. At the same time, she built Nykaa's online platform to provide convenience, variety, and quality, all of which resonated with modern consumers.

Nayar also leveraged her extensive experience in the corporate world (she was a former investment banker) to build a scalable business model with solid financial backing. Her ability to build relationships with both global and local beauty brands while ensuring quality and authenticity gave Nykaa a competitive edge over other players in the market.

Key Takeaway: Falguni Nayar's leadership at Nykaa shows how practical decision-making rooted in real-world understanding can lead to tremendous business growth. By simplifying the beauty shopping experience for her customers and providing them with quality products and expert advice, she built a business that appeals to both online and offline customers.

Final Reflections

The stories of Ritesh Agarwal, Harshil Mathur, Shashank Kumar, Vijay Shekhar Sharma, and Falguni Nayar highlight how common-sense and practicality can be powerful tools for leadership. These leaders focused on solving real-world problems with simple, actionable solutions, using common-sense as a foundation for building thriving companies. Their ability to balance simplicity with innovation and remain adaptable in the face of challenges is a testament to the importance of practical wisdom in leadership.

Reflection Questions

1. How can you simplify your leadership approach to solve real-world challenges?

2. Are you making decisions based on deep customer insights and feedback, or relying on assumptions?

3. How can you use common-sense to disrupt or innovate in your own industry?

Plan of Action

1. **Simplify Decision-Making**: Reflect on your current decision-making process. Identify areas where complexity can be reduced, and focus on what truly matters.

2. **Listen to Your Customers**: Just like the leaders mentioned above, start building a practice of listening actively to your customers. Use their feedback to drive innovation and solutions.

3. **Be Adaptive**: In today's rapidly changing business environment, adapt your leadership style to be more flexible. Look for simple, effective ways to address new challenges and capitalise on emerging trends.

> *"Great leaders don't just think outside the box;*
> *they simplify it, making the complex simple,*
> *and the simple transformative."*
> *— Ankur*

I love stories to share my message, so here are **3 more new leadership stories** featuring **Zerodha**, **Airbnb**, and **Myntra**, focusing on how these leaders have used common-sense in their leadership to build successful businesses.

8. Nithin Kamath: Zerodha's Practical Wisdom in Transforming India's Stock Market

Nithin Kamath, the founder and CEO of **Zerodha**, India's largest stock broking firm, is a stellar example of how common-sense can drive change in a highly complex and traditional industry. When Kamath started Zerodha in 2010, the Indian stock market was largely dominated by legacy brokers who charged high commissions and offered complicated platforms. The average retail investor found it difficult to engage with the stock market, often being deterred by complex processes and hidden fees.

Kamath, with his pragmatic approach, realised that the market needed to be democratised for the average person. He understood that high commissions were a barrier for retail investors to enter the stock market and that a simplified, transparent model was key to growth. Zerodha eliminated traditional brokerage fees and introduced a flat-fee structure, which was a game-changer for Indian retail investors. Additionally, they built an intuitive platform that simplified the process of trading, making it accessible to first time investors.

Zerodha's success lies in Kamath's ability to look at a complex system (stock trading) and make it simpler, more transparent, and more accessible, all based on practical wisdom and common-sense thinking. Kamath also focused on educating his customers, creating free content to help them understand the nuances of trading, further empowering the retail investor.

Key Takeaway: Nithin Kamath's leadership demonstrates how simplifying an overly complex industry and focusing on the customer's needs can disrupt the status quo. Zerodha's growth is a result of practical, common-sense leadership that prioritised transparency, simplicity, and customer empowerment.

9. Brian Chesky: Airbnb's Leadership Through Common-Sense Innovation

Brian Chesky, the co-founder and CEO of **Airbnb**, has successfully built one of the most disruptive companies in the hospitality industry by applying practical wisdom and common-sense. In the mid-2000s, Chesky and his co-founders Joe Gebbia and Nathan Blecharczyk were struggling to pay their rent in San Francisco. Instead of searching for a traditional solution, they came up with an unconventional idea—renting out air mattresses in their apartment to conference attendees who couldn't find accommodation.

The brilliance of Chesky's leadership lies in his ability to see a gap in the market and create a simple solution. Airbnb tapped into the power of the **sharing economy**, allowing individuals to rent out their spaces directly to guests, thereby cutting out traditional hotel middlemen and offering travellers unique, affordable experiences. Chesky's approach was not about reinventing the wheel but rather simplifying the idea of "home-sharing" and building a platform that connected homeowners with travellers in an easy and transparent way.

Throughout Airbnb's journey, Chesky continued to apply common-sense by focusing on creating trust and safety within the community. He introduced measures like host verification and guest reviews, which were essential in building confidence in the new business model. This focus on safety and transparency has been a key element in Airbnb's massive success.

Key Takeaway: Brian Chesky's leadership showcases how common-sense innovation can disrupt an entire industry. By simplifying the process of booking short-term stays and building trust within the community, he turned a small idea into a global business.

10. Mukesh Bansal: Myntra's Evolution through Simple Customer-Centric Decisions

Mukesh Bansal, the co-founder of **Myntra**, one of India's leading e-commerce platforms for fashion and lifestyle, has used practical wisdom and common-sense to lead Myntra through various stages of growth. Myntra started as a small online custom t-shirt business in 2007 before evolving into an online fashion giant. Bansal's leadership is a prime example of how common-sense and a deep understanding of consumer behaviour can drive success in a rapidly changing market.

When Bansal and his co-founders launched Myntra, they saw a gap in the Indian market: the lack of access to branded clothing in small cities and towns. They simplified the shopping experience by offering a wide variety of fashion products online and focusing on delivering a seamless, customer-centric experience. Myntra's early success came from addressing real pain points—offering convenience, a broad selection, and delivering orders directly to the doorstep.

What sets Bansal apart as a leader is his ability to keep things simple and focus on what truly matters to customers. Myntra's early investments in customer service, returns policy, and fast delivery were all grounded in common-sense leadership. Furthermore, Bansal made the bold decision to pivot Myntra's business model, transforming it into a platform where fashion brands could directly sell to consumers. This was a game-changing move that accelerated Myntra's growth and led to its eventual acquisition by Flipkart.

Key Takeaway: Mukesh Bansal's leadership exemplifies how understanding customer needs and focusing on simplicity and convenience can turn an idea into a market leader. His ability to navigate changing market conditions while keeping the business model simple and customer-focused has been key to Myntra's success.

Final Reflections

The leadership stories of **Nithin Kamath**, **Brian Chesky**, and **Mukesh Bansal** highlight how common-sense plays a pivotal role in navigating challenges and making practical decisions that lead to innovation and growth. These leaders didn't rely on complex strategies but focused on simplifying processes, solving real-world problems, and building trust with their customers.

By embracing practical wisdom and staying grounded in simple, effective solutions, these leaders have created businesses that are not only successful but also transformative in their respective industries. Whether it's disrupting traditional stock trading with Zerodha, reinventing travel with Airbnb, or revolutionising online fashion retail with Myntra, their leadership exemplifies the power of common-sense in the modern business world.

Reflection Questions

1. In what areas of your business or personal life could simplifying a complex process create more value?

2. How can you build more trust with your team or customers by focusing on common-sense solutions?

3. How can you embrace a "simpler is better" approach in your leadership style to drive better results?

Plan of Action

1. **Identify Opportunities for Simplicity**: Look at your current business processes and identify areas where complexity can be reduced. Simplify offerings to deliver value more efficiently.

2. **Focus on Customer Needs**: Spend time listening to your customers and understanding their pain points. Use that information to create simple solutions that directly address their needs.

3. **Build Trust Through Transparency**: Make your communication transparent, clear, and consistent. Trust is built when people know they can rely on you for straightforward, honest interactions.

> *"Great leaders know that simplicity is the foundation of success; when you make things simple, the path forward becomes clearer for everyone."*
> *— Vandana*

Chapter 16

Everyday Wisdom for a Better Tomorrow

"The future belongs to those who apply their wisdom today."
– Vandana

In the face of rapid global changes, economic uncertainties, and shifting social dynamics, many of us are often searching for the tools to navigate a better future. Amid all the complexities of the modern world, the most enduring and valuable tool at our disposal remains simple yet profound: **common-sense**. In this chapter, we explore how applying everyday wisdom—rooted in practicality, empathy, and awareness—can help us build a better tomorrow, not just for ourselves but for the world at large.

The Importance of Everyday Wisdom

Common-sense, when applied wisely, is a powerful catalyst for change. It cuts through the noise, offering us practical solutions to everyday problems. By relying on **practicality**, **awareness**, and **empathy**, common-sense can guide us toward building a sustainable future in our personal lives, workplaces, and society. The beauty of everyday wisdom lies in its simplicity—yet it can shape decisions that have far-reaching effects.

Take the example of **Indra Nooyi**, former CEO of PepsiCo, whose leadership style blended empathy and common-sense to foster not only the success of the company but also its responsibility toward the environment and society. Her vision, grounded in wisdom, emphasised the need for businesses to make a positive impact. She focused on delivering performance with purpose, which led to PepsiCo's initiatives in health-conscious products and reducing environmental impact.

Like Nooyi, many of the world's most influential leaders have applied a blend of common-sense and wisdom to drive progress. However, the application of common-sense isn't limited to corporate giants. It's equally relevant in how we approach everyday challenges, whether it's navigating personal relationships, contributing to societal betterment, or making ethical choices in the face of adversity.

Practical Wisdom: A Steady Compass for Navigating Change

When we talk about **practical wisdom**, we're referring to a form of decision-making that is rooted in a deep understanding of real-life circumstances. Practical wisdom doesn't just rely on abstract ideas or theoretical knowledge—it focuses on **what works in the real-world**, given specific contexts and constraints. In a world constantly in flux, common-sense provides a steady compass to keep us grounded and guide our actions.

Practical wisdom can be seen in **Elon Musk's** decision to develop electric vehicles at **Tesla**. Despite facing immense scepticism from the automotive industry, Musk applied a simple, powerful concept: make electric cars mainstream and, in doing so, fight climate change. This decision wasn't based solely on high-tech innovations but also on common-sense—recognising that the future of the planet demanded sustainable solutions.

Similarly, **Narayana Murthy**, co-founder of **Infosys**, applied practical wisdom by democratising access to information technology in India. At a time when software services were expensive and limited to large corporations, Murthy's vision was to create a global IT powerhouse with a strong emphasis on ethical business practices. His decisions were grounded in the practical understanding that businesses can thrive while remaining true to their core values.

Empathy: The Heartbeat of Tomorrow's Success

In today's increasingly fragmented world, **empathy** has become one of the most powerful forces for creating change. Leaders who exhibit empathy do more than just show concern for others—they create an environment where people feel seen, heard, and understood. **Empathy in leadership** is more than just about caring for employees or clients; it's about **building connections** that foster trust, collaboration, and positive outcomes.

Consider the leadership of **Jacinda Ardern**, Prime Minister of New Zealand, who has demonstrated how empathetic leadership can lead to long-term positive change. Following the Christchurch mosque shootings in 2019, Ardern's response was rooted in compassion and action. Her leadership approach was simple but effective: she reached out to the victims and their families with empathy, and then made practical decisions that led to the swift reform of New Zealand's gun laws.

Ardern's leadership exemplifies how **empathy** can bridge divides and initiate meaningful societal change. In a world often divided by ideologies and misinformation, an empathetic approach can foster unity and collaboration. When leaders and individuals are willing to put themselves in others' shoes, they can inspire profound transformations, whether that's changing the direction of an organisation or fostering peace in a community.

In a corporate setting, empathy also plays a significant role. Take **Satya Nadella**, the CEO of Microsoft, whose emphasis on building an empathetic company culture has revitalised the tech giant. Under Nadella's leadership, Microsoft's focus shifted toward empathy and inclusivity, making it a better workplace for all employees. Nadella's ability to lead with compassion not only transformed Microsoft's internal culture but also drove innovative products that better served their customers' needs.

Awareness: The Foundation of Thoughtful Action

Awareness is another cornerstone of common-sense. Without awareness, it becomes difficult to make thoughtful, informed decisions. Being aware means understanding your surroundings, recognising patterns, and knowing when to act and when to pause. It requires paying attention to the present moment and the broader context, which is vital for making decisions that can benefit the future.

Take the example of **Ratan Tata**, the former chairman of **Tata Group**, who has always demonstrated an acute sense of awareness in his decision-making. Tata's leadership has been defined by an awareness of his company's social responsibilities and the long-term implications of business decisions. He made crucial decisions such as the acquisition of **Corus** and **Jaguar Land Rover**, which were based on a well-rounded understanding of global market dynamics and the need for diversification. His awareness of the importance of sustainability and ethical business practices has shaped Tata Group into one of India's most respected conglomerates.

Similarly, **Arianna Huffington**, the founder of **HuffPost**, applied awareness in her approach to health and work-life balance. Recognising the toll that burnout was taking on herself and others, Huffington shifted her focus toward well-being. She turned **Thrive Global**, a platform dedicated to well-being and productivity, into a thriving business. Her ability to recognise the challenges of the modern work environment and act on them was a perfect example of **awareness** combined with practicality.

Building a Future Rooted in Empathy, Practicality, and Awareness

Building a better tomorrow begins with small, everyday actions rooted in common-sense. It is about applying **practical wisdom** in everyday situations, showing **empathy** toward others, and maintaining a deep **awareness** of the challenges and opportunities in the world. It is about recognising that we all play a role in shaping the future, and each action we take can either contribute to or detract from the collective well-being.

This is why common-sense must be a key pillar of **future-oriented leadership**. As we face a future marked by technological disruption, environmental crises, and social inequities, the ability to approach these challenges with practical wisdom, empathy, and awareness will be crucial. **Leaders who combine these attributes can create organisations that not only survive but thrive**, contributing to a future that is equitable, sustainable, and compassionate.

Practical Tips for Building a Better Tomorrow

1. **Simplify Decision-Making**: Focus on what truly matters in any given situation. Cut through the noise and avoid over-complicating decisions. Ask yourself: "What's the most practical solution here, and how does it benefit the long-term?"

2. **Lead with Empathy**: Understand the needs and perspectives of those around you. Whether you're managing a team or contributing to your community, approach every situation with empathy, and ensure that others feel heard and valued.

3. **Cultivate Awareness**: Stay attuned to your surroundings and constantly assess the changing dynamics in your personal life and business environment. Be mindful of emerging trends, and be ready to adapt your approach based on new insights.

4. **Foster Inclusivity**: In any organisation, make sure that voices from all backgrounds are heard. Inclusivity, driven by empathy and awareness, leads to better decisions and a more harmonious environment.

5. **Commit to Continuous Learning**: The world is constantly evolving, and so must our approaches to leadership and decision-making. Stay curious and open to new ideas and feedback, and always seek to improve your judgement.

Reflection Questions

1. How can you apply more common-sense in your leadership style to create a lasting positive impact in your organisation?

2. In what ways can you cultivate empathy in your daily interactions, whether at work or in personal relationships, to foster understanding and collaboration?

3. What steps can you take today to be more aware of the broader context of your decisions and actions in both your personal and professional life?

Plan of Action

1. **Evaluate Current Decisions**: Take a moment to evaluate the decisions you've made recently. Were they grounded in common-sense? Could you have approached them with more practicality, empathy, or awareness? Make note of areas where you can improve.

2. **Practice Active Listening**: Start incorporating more listening into your leadership approach. Pay attention to the needs, concerns, and feelings of those around you, whether they're colleagues, family members, or clients. Be genuinely present in conversations.

3. **Focus on the Long-Term**: Consider how your actions today will impact the future. Whether it's in your career, business, or personal life, ensure that your decisions are aligned with long-term values and objectives.

"A better tomorrow begins with the wisdom
we apply today. Lead with practicality, empathy,
and awareness, and the future will unfold in
ways we can all be proud of."
– Vandana

Chapter 17

Rediscovering the Art of Common-Sense

"Common-sense is the foundation of all human wisdom.
It is not something you can learn in books,
but rather something that comes from experience,
observation, and reflection."
– Vandana

In a world that is increasingly driven by complexity, technology, and fast-paced changes, the simple yet profound art of common-sense has been overshadowed. We are bombarded with information, advised by countless experts, and presented with solutions to every problem imaginable. But in the midst of this information overload, common-sense—perhaps the most essential tool for navigating life—has often been relegated to the background.

However, rediscovering the art of common-sense is not only important, it is vital. Common-sense, when practiced consciously, is the key to making better decisions, fostering deeper relationships, and driving meaningful change. In this chapter, we will take a reflective journey through the lessons we've learned about common-sense and explore how we can embrace it as a powerful skill to live a more meaningful life.

The Lost Art: Common-Sense in a Modern World

Common-sense may be seen as an ancient virtue, but it remains relevant in today's digital world. It's not about being simplistic or naive, but rather about approaching situations with clarity, practicality, and sound judgement. In a time when specialisation often overshadows general knowledge, and data-driven solutions cloud our understanding of human needs, common-sense can cut through the noise and help us make grounded decisions.

Consider the example of **Howard Schultz**, the former CEO of Starbucks, who, in the midst of expanding his company globally, never lost sight of the basic principles that made Starbucks successful. He always emphasised the importance of human connection and customer experience—basic principles of common-sense that many businesses overlook in favour of technology or the latest trends. Schultz's emphasis on **creating an emotional connection with customers** and fostering a sense of belonging is a perfect example of how common-sense can guide business decisions that resonate on a human level.

Schultz's story serves as a reminder that common-sense is not about following the most popular trend or relying on the newest technology, but rather about sticking to what works at a fundamental level: understanding people and the simple things that make life better.

"The greatest enemy of knowledge is not ignorance,
it is the illusion of knowledge"
– Stephen Hawking

The Core Principles of Common-Sense

Through the exploration of common-sense in various chapters, we've uncovered several essential principles that form the backbone of this skill. Let's summarise these key takeaways and lessons that will help you rediscover the art of common-sense.

1. **Practicality Over Perfection**: One of the most valuable aspects of common-sense is its focus on practicality. In a world where we are often taught to aim for perfection, common-sense reminds us that **doing what is realistic and achievable** is often more important than striving for an unattainable ideal. Think of **Jack Ma**, the founder of Alibaba. When he started his e-commerce empire, he faced countless setbacks and challenges. Yet, instead of chasing perfection, he focused on **solving real problems** for people, such as providing small businesses access to online markets. His focus on practical solutions helped him build one of the world's most valuable companies.

2. **Emotional Intelligence**: Common-sense goes hand-in-hand with **emotional intelligence**—the ability to recognise and understand your own emotions and those of others. This is particularly evident in leadership. Consider **Oprah Winfrey**, whose empathy and emotional intelligence have made her an influential figure. Oprah didn't just build a media empire; she built relationships by applying common-sense in understanding the human condition. By showing genuine care for people and **recognising the power of human connection**, Oprah created an empire that resonates deeply with millions.

3. **Simplicity Over Complexity**: Common-sense encourages simplicity. In a world full of noise, we often overcomplicate our decisions, thinking that more is better. However, **simplicity is**

often the key to clarity. Think of **Steve Jobs**, the co-founder of Apple. Jobs was a master of reducing complexity to create simple, user-friendly products. The **iPhone**, for instance, revolutionised the way we interact with technology, precisely because it simplified a complicated process into something intuitive and easy to use. Jobs' focus on simplicity was rooted in common-sense—design that serves real human needs without overwhelming us with unnecessary features.

4. **Decision-Making Based on Sound Judgement**: Common-sense relies on judgement—knowing when to act, when to wait, and when to seek counsel. **Bill Gates**, the co-founder of Microsoft, has often made decisions based on sound judgement, such as the early decision to partner with IBM and adapt Windows as a system that could be installed on many PCs. Gates understood the need for **flexibility and scalability** in his business. His judgement wasn't based on what others were doing, but on what made sense for the business, its users, and its potential for growth.

5. **Actionable Knowledge**: Common-sense is not just theoretical; it's about **actionable knowledge**. It's about knowing what to do with what you know. Take **Mukesh Ambani**, the chairman of Reliance Industries, as an example. His move into the telecom industry with **Jio** was a strategic move based on common-sense. He saw an opportunity to democratise access to digital technology in India, providing affordable internet to millions. His decision wasn't driven by fancy technologies or trends but by a **deep understanding of India's needs and the practical application of technology to solve a major problem**.

Embracing Common-Sense as a Skill

Common-sense is often perceived as a natural quality, something that some people simply have and others don't. But the truth is, common-sense can and should be nurtured as a **skill**. It's a skill that requires practice, self-awareness, and a commitment to learning from experience. Here's how you can begin to develop common-sense in your own life.

1. **Slow Down and Reflect**: In today's fast-paced world, we're often caught up in the rush of daily life. Common-sense requires taking the time to pause, reflect, and understand the situation before acting. In every situation, ask yourself: "What is the simplest solution here? What is the most practical course of action?"

2. **Learn from Your Mistakes**: Common-sense comes from **experience**—and often, experience means making mistakes. The key is to learn from those mistakes and adjust your approach accordingly. Consider **Edison's approach to invention**: he famously said, "I have not failed. I've just found 10,000 ways that won't work." His approach to failure was grounded in common-sense—he viewed every mistake as an opportunity to learn and improve.

3. **Focus on What's Important**: In the hustle of everyday life, we often get distracted by trivial things. **Common-sense** requires us to focus on what matters and ignore distractions. In business, this might mean focusing on delivering value to customers rather than chasing every new trend. In relationships, it might mean valuing **quality over quantity** in interactions. Focus on **what truly adds value** in your life and eliminate what doesn't.

4. **Cultivate Emotional Awareness**: The ability to read emotional cues and respond appropriately is a vital aspect of common-sense. Whether it's in a personal relationship or a business interaction, **empathy and emotional intelligence** are powerful tools for navigating complex situations. By developing a deeper understanding of emotions, you can make better decisions that benefit everyone involved.

5. **Question Your Assumptions**: Common-sense involves **critical thinking**—the ability to question assumptions and evaluate the best course of action. Don't rely on what seems like the obvious choice; instead, challenge your own thinking. Ask yourself: "Is this truly the best option, or am I missing something?" This mindset of curiosity and questioning will help you hone your decision-making skills.

The Future of Common-Sense

In a world where we're constantly bombarded by information and technological advancements, **common-sense is more important than ever**. The ability to use **practical wisdom** in combination with **emotional intelligence** and **critical thinking** is key to navigating our complex world. The future will demand more leaders who are grounded in common-sense, who can balance technological innovations with human needs, and who can make decisions that are both practical and empathetic.

As the world continues to evolve, we must **rediscover** the timeless art of common-sense—applying it in new ways to solve the challenges of tomorrow. By **embracing common-sense as a skill**, we can create a better, more sustainable future for ourselves, our businesses, and our communities.

Reflection Questions

1. How have you applied common-sense in your life or career so far? What decisions have you made that have been grounded in practicality, empathy, and awareness?

2. In what areas of your life do you feel you could benefit from a more common-sense approach? What practical steps can you take to cultivate this skill?

3. How can you teach the next generation to embrace common-sense as a key life skill, especially in a world that often values speed and complexity over simplicity and wisdom?

Plan of Action

1. **Identify Areas for Practical Wisdom**: Look at your current challenges and identify areas where a more **practical, grounded approach** could help. This could be in decision-making, personal relationships, or work-related situations.

2. **Practice Reflection**: Set aside time each day or week for quiet reflection. Consider how you've approached recent situations and whether a more **common-sense approach** might have yielded better results.

3. **Develop Emotional Intelligence**: Focus on **deepening your emotional awareness** in your interactions. Practice listening more actively and responding with empathy. This will help you apply common-sense in a more balanced, thoughtful way.

"The power of common-sense is not in how much
we know but in how wisely we apply what we know."
– Vandana

Chapter 18

Your Common-Sense Toolkit

"Common-sense is not so common."
– Voltaire

In a world full of distractions, rapid technological advancements, and a constant bombardment of information, the ability to apply common-sense can often feel elusive. Yet, it is the fundamental skill that allows us to make grounded, practical decisions in both our personal and professional lives. Common-sense is not just about innate wisdom—it's a skill that can be cultivated and nurtured through intention, practice, and continuous learning.

In this chapter, we will build your **Common-Sense Toolkit**, equipping you with practical exercises and habits to develop this invaluable skill. We will also introduce a **30-day action plan** that will guide you in integrating this wisdom into your daily life. If common-sense is the foundation of effective decision-making and meaningful living, then this toolkit will help you become a master builder of your future.

The Importance of Mastering Common-Sense

Before we dive into the toolkit, let's revisit why mastering common-sense is so crucial. The modern world is filled with complexity, distractions, and noise. Every day, we are faced with countless decisions—big and small—many of which demand clarity, wisdom, and thoughtful consideration. The ability to act with common-sense allows us to:

1. **Make Better Decisions**: Whether you're navigating personal challenges or professional dilemmas, common-sense helps you choose the most practical course of action based on **sound judgement** and **realistic expectations**.

2. **Build Stronger Relationships**: Common-sense is at the heart of emotional intelligence, empathy, and clear communication— essential components for healthy relationships in both personal and professional spheres.

3. **Simplify Complex Problems**: In a world full of information overload, common-sense allows us to cut through the noise and **focus on what truly matters**, solving problems in the most efficient and effective way.

4. **Adapt to Change**: As change continues to accelerate in the world around us, the ability to apply common-sense enables us to **stay grounded**, stay **calm**, and make decisions that are aligned with our values, even in uncertain times.

By intentionally developing common-sense, you're not just improving your ability to make decisions—you're enhancing your life's quality by becoming more attuned to the world around you.

Building Your Common-Sense Toolkit

Now, let's explore the tools and exercises that will help you develop the core components of common-sense: clarity, empathy, simplicity, emotional intelligence, and sound judgement. Each of these tools is essential in strengthening your ability to act with wisdom, practicality, and awareness.

1. The Power of Reflection: Daily Journaling:

Common-sense often comes from **self-awareness**—being aware of your thoughts, emotions, actions, and the results they produce. One powerful way to develop this awareness is through **daily journaling**.

Exercise: Every day, set aside 10–15 minutes to write about your experiences. Ask yourself these questions as prompts for reflection:

- What decisions did I make today? How did I approach them?

- What worked well, and what could I have done differently?

- Was there a situation where I could have been more practical or grounded in my approach?

By making this a daily habit, you will begin to uncover patterns in your thinking and decision-making process. You'll start to recognise areas where you tend to overthink or complicate things unnecessarily. This insight will help you sharpen your common-sense muscle and develop more practical solutions in the future.

2. Cultivating Empathy: The Power of Listening:

One of the cornerstones of common-sense is the ability to **understand and connect with others**. Empathy plays a significant role in how we approach situations and make decisions, especially in relationships and leadership.

Exercise: For the next week, practice **active listening** with those around you. In every conversation, **listen more than you speak**.

Focus on understanding the other person's perspective before offering your own thoughts. This will help you:

- Gain insights into others' emotions and needs.

- Avoid rushing to judgement or reacting impulsively.

- Respond with more **practicality and empathy**.

Empathy allows you to take in all the necessary information and view situations from a broader perspective, which ultimately helps you make decisions that are grounded in common-sense.

3. Emotional Intelligence: The Art of Self-Regulation:

Self-regulation—the ability to manage your emotions and reactions—is a critical aspect of common-sense. Emotional intelligence is the foundation for **wise decision-making** because it allows you to **respond thoughtfully** rather than reacting impulsively based on emotion.

Exercise: When faced with an emotional reaction (whether it's frustration, anger, or excitement), practice the following:

- **Pause**: Take a deep breath and allow yourself a moment of reflection.

- **Reflect**: Ask yourself, "What is causing this emotion? How can I respond in a way that is practical and aligned with my goals?"

- **Respond**: Choose your response carefully, based on clarity and rational thought rather than being driven solely by emotion.

This simple practice will help you regulate your emotions in the heat of the moment and improve your decision-making capacity.

4. Critical Thinking: The Questioning Mindset:

Common-sense is rooted in the ability to **think critically**—to question assumptions and evaluate the situation from all angles before making decisions. The ability to think critically leads to better judgement and wiser choices.

Exercise: Before making any significant decision, take time to ask the following **critical questions**:

- What are the potential risks and benefits of this decision?

- Are there alternative solutions or approaches that might be more effective?

- What are the short-term and long-term implications of my choice?

By regularly asking these questions, you train your mind to not only think logically but also act in a more **practical, solution-focused** way. This practice can be applied to both personal and professional situations, allowing you to make decisions based on critical thinking and sound judgement.

5. Simplification: The Art of Clarity:

In a world full of noise and complexity, one of the best ways to apply common-sense is to simplify the situation. Often, the most practical solution is the simplest one. Common-sense thrives in simplicity—finding clear, straightforward solutions rather than over-complicating things.

Exercise: For the next 30 days, practice **simplifying** your approach to problem-solving. Break down complex issues into manageable steps:

- Identify the core issue.

- Eliminate unnecessary steps or actions.

- Focus on practical, actionable solutions that address the problem directly.

This approach will help you eliminate confusion and move forward with greater clarity and confidence.

The Benefits of Cultivating Common-Sense

Why invest time and effort in mastering common-sense? The answer lies in the transformative impact it can have on your life.

In Personal Life

- **Better Decision-Making:** Practical wisdom helps navigate daily challenges with clarity.

- **Problem-Solving:** It sharpens your ability to find effective solutions to life's hurdles.

- **Stronger Relationships:** Empathy and understanding foster healthier connections.

- **In Professional Life**

- **Enhanced Leadership:** Common-sense empowers leaders to guide teams with pragmatism.

- **Adaptability:** It fosters flexibility, making you resilient in dynamic environments.

- **Conflict Resolution:** Practical wisdom aids in finding win-win solutions in workplace disputes.

- **In Spiritual Life**

- **Ethical Choices:** Common-sense aligns actions with values, fostering integrity.

- **Mindfulness:** It encourages living in the moment and appreciating life's simplicity.

- **Compassion:** Practical wisdom deepens empathy, connecting you to the greater good.

Your 30-Day Action Plan: Integrating Common-Sense into Daily Life

Now that you have the tools to develop common-sense, it's time to put them into action. Here's a **30-day action plan** to help you integrate these habits into your daily life. Each day will focus on one exercise or habit that will build your common-sense muscle and help you create a more practical, thoughtful, and grounded life.

Week 1: **Building Awareness and Reflection**

- **Day 1-3**: Start your daily journaling practice. Write for 10-15 minutes each day.

- **Day 4-7**: Practice **active listening** in all your conversations. Focus on understanding the other person's perspective.

Week 2: **Developing Emotional Intelligence**

- **Day 8-10**: Practice **self-regulation** by pausing before reacting emotionally. Reflect before responding.

- **Day 11-14**: Engage in deep self-reflection. Write about how you've managed emotions in challenging situations.

Week 3: **Sharpening Critical Thinking and Simplification**

- **Day 15-17**: Start asking **critical questions** before making important decisions. Record your reflections in your journal.

- **Day 18-21**: Simplify a complex task or problem. Break it down into smaller, more manageable steps.

Week 4: **Integrating Practical Wisdom into Your Life**

- **Day 22-24**: Focus on making practical, grounded decisions at work or home. Reflect on your decision-making process.

- **Day 25-28**: Practice simplifying a recurring problem. Identify a solution that is efficient and simple.

- **Day 29-30**: Reflect on the past month. How have these practices helped you make wiser decisions and live with more common-sense?

Reflection Questions for the End of Your 30-Day Plan

1. What has been the most surprising insight you gained about yourself during this 30-day process?

2. In what areas of your life do you feel more grounded and practical after practicing common-sense?

3. How will you continue to nurture and apply common-sense moving forward?

Plan of Action for the Future

1. **Continue Journaling**: Keep the habit of daily reflection to stay connected with your inner wisdom.

2. **Practice Active Listening**: Make it a regular habit to listen deeply in all interactions, improving empathy and understanding.

3. **Commit to Simplicity**: In every aspect of life, aim to find the simplest, most practical solution.

4. **Refine Your Decision-Making**: Use critical thinking and common-sense regularly to make informed, grounded decisions.

"The mastery of common-sense comes not from knowing everything but from knowing how to approach life with clarity, practicality, and wisdom."
—Vandana

Sharing my life stories

Uncommon Beginnings:
A Story of Common-Sense

Let me take you back to 1979, a year etched in my memory as the beginning of something profound. I was just a five-year-old when my father suffered a life-altering accident. But this story isn't just about adversity—it's about resilience, love, and the birth of my most enduring life skill: **common-sense.**

Before this pivotal moment, my parents had already defied societal norms. In 1971, they chose love over expectations, marrying across castes in a world that didn't easily forgive such choices. This decision came with its own costs—chiefly, the lack of a traditional family support system. So, when my father's accident happened, we were left to fend for ourselves.

My mother, however, was a force of nature. A fantastic cook, she transformed our home into a haven for intern doctors who sought comfort in her meals. On the surface, it seemed like a practical solution to keep us afloat. But beneath the surface, something extraordinary was brewing.

The Makeshift Kitchen That Shaped My Soul

Our kitchen wasn't just a place where food was prepared—it became my classroom for life. As my mom balanced taking care of my injured father, running a home, and ensuring we kids stayed in school, I found myself her unlikely little assistant.

There were no toys to distract me, no carefree childhood moments. Instead, there were decisions to be made, chores to complete, and lessons to absorb. At the time, I didn't realise what was happening. I was simply doing what needed to be done. But looking back now, I see that these moments were quietly shaping my character, teaching me the essence of common-sense:

- **Adaptability:** When life throws you a curveball, you find ways to catch it.

- **Responsibility:** Even a five-year-old can contribute meaningfully when necessity demands it.

- **Resilience:** The ability to thrive amid challenges was being sown in my spirit.

Connecting the Dots

Steve Jobs famously said, *"You can't connect the dots looking forward; you can only connect them looking backward."* As I reflect on those early years, I see how the dots align. My successes today—the decisions I make, the challenges I overcome—are deeply rooted in the lessons learned in that makeshift kitchen.

Common-sense became my silent guide, a thread of grounded wisdom running through every twist and turn of life. It didn't come from books or classrooms but from the raw, unfiltered reality of growing up in a home that turned adversity into opportunity.

Common-sense is the collection of
prejudices acquired by age 18.
– Albert Einstein

Reflections on Common-Sense

What does common-sense mean to you?

For me, it has been both a compass and a lifeline. Growing up in a multicultural environment, I realised common-sense transcends boundaries, acting as a unifying thread among diverse perspectives.

It is this grounded reasoning that has helped me navigate life's complexities—whether as a child stepping into adult responsibilities or as an adult seeking clarity in chaotic situations.

A Question for You

What challenges have you faced that inadvertently nurtured your common-sense, becoming the silent force guiding your decisions?

Timeless Wisdom on Common-Sense

"Common-sense is the genius of humanity."
– Johann Wolfgang von Goethe

In our journey together, let common-sense be our guiding star—a light that transforms the ordinary into the extraordinary and reveals the profound in the obvious.

"In the ordinary, find the extraordinary.
In the obvious, discover the profound".
– Vandana

Your Turn

What does common-sense mean to you, and how will you cultivate it as a skill that propels you toward personal, professional, and spiritual excellence?

This is your story to write. Let's begin.

The Lone Rebel:
Growing Through Unconventional Choices

Reflecting on a moment of rebellion in my life feels like opening a chapter titled, **"The Lone Rebel."** It's a story of standing alone, of swimming against the tide—not for the sake of defiance, but for something deeper: a commitment to doing what is right.

The Professional Crossroads

In my professional journey, I often found myself faced with a choice: follow the path of least resistance or stand firm for what I believed in. One such defining moment occurred during the testing phase of a product I was responsible for.

I spotted critical issues that, if overlooked, could compromise the user experience and the integrity of the product. But here's the catch: acknowledging these issues meant delays, more work, and potential friction with senior management.

The "practical" choice, as others saw it, was to let it slide— pass the test case and move on. But for me, that wasn't an option. Common-sense told me that short-term convenience could never outweigh long-term repercussions.

The Rebel's Stand

I raised my concerns, explaining the risks of ignoring the issues. What followed was a series of lengthy email exchanges with project leaders and senior management. The pushback was intense.

"Why can't you just let it go?"

"This is how things are done."

"Don't complicate the process."

But I refused to back down. Alone in my corner, I fought for what I believed was right—for the users who would interact with the product, for the trust that good work demands.

It wasn't easy. I wasn't seeking to curry favour with my managers or secure better appraisal ratings. I was guided by a higher principle: integrity.

The Outcome and the Lessons

After weeks of discussions and persistence, my concerns were validated. The issues I raised were addressed, and the product improved. The battle had been worth it—not just for the outcome but for the lessons it taught me:

- **Resilience**: Standing firm in the face of opposition strengthens your resolve.

- **Purpose**: When your actions are guided by a greater purpose, they carry more weight.

- **Growth**: Nonconformity pushes you out of your comfort zone, helping you grow.

Common-Sense Through Nonconformity

In hindsight, these moments of rebellion were less about defiance and more about clarity. They became stepping stones in developing a form of **common-sense** that goes beyond the obvious. It's the kind of common-sense that challenges assumptions, questions norms, and prioritises long-term value over short-term ease.

A Question for Reflection

What's one moment in your life where you chose to stand alone, and how did it shape your journey?

The Courage to Be a Common-Sense Rebel

True growth often lies beyond the boundaries of conformity. When you dare to challenge the norm and embrace the harder path, you uncover not only your own strength but also the extraordinary within you.

> *"Dare to be a rebel of common-sense,*
> *for in your defiance, you may forge a path*
> *that others will follow."*
> *– Vandana*

How can you integrate this mindset of nonconformity into your approach to common-sense, shaping it into a skill that transforms not only your life but the lives of others?

Blending Ethics and Common-Sense: A Diamond-Solid Foundation

Let me share a real-life moment where ethics and common-sense converged, becoming the foundation for an unwavering commitment to integrity.

In the intricate world of diamonds and deadlines, I once faced a dilemma that tested both my values and decision-making. A customer ordered exquisite diamond bangles—crafted with the promise of impeccable VVS-GH quality—for her daughter's wedding. It was a project where trust was as critical as craftsmanship.

Hours before delivery, a revelation from the certification lab shook me: 15 out of 100 diamonds in one bangle didn't meet the promised quality. The clock was ticking, the wedding was imminent, and I stood at a crossroad:

- **Option 1:** Deliver as-is, hope no one notices, and meet the deadline.

- **Option 2:** Disclose the issue, risk angering the customer, and miss the deadline.

Convenience pointed toward Option 1, but my common-sense and ethical compass steered me to Option 2. Deception wasn't an option—not when integrity is the bedrock of who I am.

We informed the customer, explained the situation transparently, and offered a solution: proceed with the current bangles for the wedding and replace the diamonds afterward. Understandably, the customer was initially upset. However, once we shared our honesty and assurance, they appreciated the integrity and chose to continue the relationship.

This story isn't about diamonds—it's about the priceless value of trust. In a business where transparency can be as rare as flawless gems, my decision reinforced a vital principle: doing what's right is always worth more than taking the easy way out.

The Intersection of Common-Sense and Ethics

This experience taught me that common-sense is more than practical reasoning—it's the bridge between our ethical ideals and real-world actions. Ethics, when illuminated by common-sense, becomes the compass that helps us navigate dilemmas with clarity and compassion.

As Thomas Jefferson wisely said:

> *"In matters of style, swim with the current;*
> *in matters of principle,*
> *stand like a rock."*

Your Turn to Reflect

What crossroads have you faced where common-sense and ethics guided your decisions? How can you let integrity illuminate your actions, even when the path is tough?

Integrity, after all, isn't just a choice—it's a lifestyle. One that resonates not only with others but with the truest version of yourself.

Navigating Crisis:
Common-Sense and Rational Thinking
as Our Compass

Entrepreneurship has been an exhilarating journey for both of us—a dynamic duo fuelled by passion, creativity, and the combined power of common-sense and rational thinking. Together, we've ventured into 7 diverse businesses. Some soared, others found new owners, and a few met their inevitable closures.

Here's a glimpse into our ventures that didn't make it to the finish line:

1. **Talent Time (Hobby Studio) – 2008:** Closed, No Profit/No Loss

2. **Food & Beverages – 2012:** Sold at 10% Profit

3. **Luxury Gifting Boutique – 2013:** Closed, No Profit/No Loss

4. **Apparels Showroom – 2014:** Hard Shut, Failed Business, Lost a Quarter Million

Each venture was born from enthusiasm, yet not all were destined to thrive. What anchored us during these turbulent times was our shared belief: *Don't treat your business like a baby*. This principle enabled us to make tough decisions without emotional entanglements, balancing Vandana's intuitive common-sense with Ankur's logical reasoning.

Talent Time: A Joint Decision to Celebrate and Move Forward

One of our most memorable ventures was *Talent Time*, a hobby studio designed to help parents nurture their children's talents. While the concept was well-intentioned, we faced challenges in gaining the appreciation and understanding we had hoped for from our customers.

Ankur's rational mind weighed the operational costs, and Vandana's common-sense whispered, "This isn't aligning with our vision." Together, we decided to close the studio, but not without celebrating its successes. We hosted a final showcase event, giving closure not only to ourselves but also to our community. Some customers protested, but we stood united, refunded any dues, and moved forward with invaluable lessons.

The Ethnic Boutique: A Strategic Exit Plan

Our ethnic party wear boutique started strong, with a prime location and promising demand. Yet, something felt amiss. Vandana's intuitive sense flagged the disconnect, while Ankur's rational analysis confirmed the financial challenges.

Rather than prolong the struggle, we devised a strategic exit plan. We liquidated the stock with irresistible offers, ensuring a clean break before the lease renewal. The remaining inventory turned into thoughtful gifts for loved ones and house help—a pragmatic and heartfelt conclusion to this chapter.

The Power of Our Partnership in Crisis

During crises, our differing perspectives became our greatest strength. Vandana's common-sense brought clarity to immediate challenges, while Ankur's rational thinking provided structure and long-term foresight. Together, we navigated the crossroads of right versus convenient, always choosing integrity and resilience.

> *"In the eye of the storm, common-sense is the compass*
> *that guides us through tumultuous seas, steering*
> *us towards safety and clarity"*
> *– Ankur*

Your Reflection Point

Have you ever faced a tough decision where both intuition and logic were needed? Could a balance of perspectives help you find clarity in such moments?

As co-founders and partners in life, we've learned that entrepreneurship isn't just about celebrating wins; it's about knowing when to pivot, when to let go, and when to lean on each other's strengths. After all, every ending is simply the beginning of another adventure.

Recommended Reading on Common-Sense and Practical Wisdom

To deepen your understanding and further develop your common-sense skills, here are some insightful books and articles that focus on practical wisdom, critical thinking, emotional intelligence, and decision-making:

1. **"The Art of Thinking Clearly" by Rolf Dobelli**

   - This book provides a fascinating collection of cognitive biases and logical fallacies, helping you develop clearer thinking patterns and avoid common mistakes in judgement.

2. **"Thinking, Fast and Slow" by Daniel Kahneman**

   - Nobel laureate Daniel Kahneman explores the 2 systems of thinking: the fast, intuitive one and the slow, deliberate one. Understanding these systems can greatly improve your ability to make rational, practical decisions.

3. **"The Wisdom of Insecurity: A Message for an Age of Anxiety" by Alan Watts**

   - Watts argues for living in the present moment and embracing uncertainty, offering a philosophical perspective that aligns with common-sense wisdom in navigating life's challenges.

4. **"Blink: The Power of Thinking Without Thinking" by Malcolm Gladwell**

   - Gladwell delves into the unconscious biases and rapid judgements that shape decision-making, emphasising the importance of trusting your instincts when informed by experience.

5. **"Emotional Intelligence: Why It Can Matter More Than IQ" by Daniel Goleman**

   - This book emphasises the critical role of emotional intelligence in decision-making, leadership, and relationships—skills integral to practicing common-sense.

6. **"The 7 Habits of Highly Effective People" by Stephen R. Covey**

   - Covey's work focuses on personal growth, leadership, and decision-making, with a focus on principles and timeless wisdom that can be applied practically in day-to-day life.

7. **"Common-Sense" by Thomas Paine**

   - This classic pamphlet, written in the 18th century, still offers valuable lessons in the importance of clarity and practical thinking in the face of complex issues, particularly in politics.

8. **"The Practical Wisdom of the Ages" by J. Donald Walters**

   - A collection of wisdom from diverse traditions and cultures, providing guidance on how to live thoughtfully and practically, grounded in timeless principles.

9. **"The Paradox of Choice: Why More Is Less" by Barry Schwartz**

   - Schwartz explores how having too many choices leads to confusion and dissatisfaction, urging a more practical, less-overwhelming approach to decision-making.

10. **"Grit: The Power of Passion and Perseverance" by Angela Duckworth**

   - Duckworth explores the power of grit—passion and perseverance—and how common-sense can help you keep a steady course through challenges, using both practicality and resilience.

Worksheets for Strengthening Observation, Thinking, and Awareness

---

These worksheets are designed to guide you in strengthening the key components of common-sense: observation, thinking, and awareness. Use these exercises regularly to build your ability to make grounded, practical decisions.

Worksheet 1: Strengthening Observation Skills

Objective: To improve your ability to notice details and gather essential information to make better decisions.

1. **Practice Active Observation**: Spend 10 minutes today observing your surroundings. Write down what you see, hear, smell, and feel.

   - What is one thing that stands out that you hadn't noticed before?

   - How does this observation help you make a more informed decision in the future?

2. **Mindful Observation Exercise**: Take a walk and observe everything around you as if you're seeing it for the first time. Focus on noticing things you usually overlook (colours, shapes, sounds, textures).

   - What new insights did you gain by being mindful in your observation?

   - How can this practice influence your decision-making process?

3. **Reflection**: At the end of the day, reflect on a situation where you could have benefited from better observation.

   - What did you overlook?

   - How can you apply more mindful observation next time?

Worksheet 2: Strengthening Critical Thinking

Objective: To enhance your ability to think clearly and make sound decisions.

1. **Identify the Problem**: Write down a current challenge or decision you're facing.

   - What are the core issues you need to address?

   - What assumptions are you making about this situation?

2. **List Possible Solutions**: For each possible solution, list the benefits and risks involved.

   - Which solution aligns best with your values and practical goals?

   - Which solution will yield the most effective long-term results?

3. **Consider Alternative Perspectives**: Seek advice from someone you trust. What would they say about this decision? Write their advice.

- How does their perspective change your view on the issue?
- What practical advice can you apply from this conversation?

Worksheet 3: Strengthening Self-Awareness

Objective: To increase your awareness of your emotional triggers and decision-making tendencies.

1. **Identify Emotional Triggers**: Write down 3 situations where you felt a strong emotional reaction recently (e.g., anger, frustration, excitement).

- What was the situation?
- What emotions did you experience, and why do you think you reacted that way?

2. **Reflect on the Outcome**: For each situation, how did your emotions influence your decision-making?

- Was the decision made based on common-sense or impulse?
- How could you have used more practical judgement?

3. **Create a Plan for Self-Regulation**: For each emotional trigger, identify a strategy for responding more thoughtfully next time.

- What self-regulation techniques can you use to keep calm and clear-headed (e.g., deep breathing, pausing, journaling)?

Worksheet 4: Strengthening Practical Wisdom

Objective: To apply common-sense to real-life situations by taking a practical approach to problem-solving.

1. **List a Current Problem**: Write down a problem you're facing, either at work or in your personal life.

   - What are the immediate, practical solutions that come to mind?
   - What is the simplest and most effective course of action?

2. **Consider the Long-Term Effects**: For each solution, consider how it will affect you in the long-term.

   - Does it align with your values and priorities?
   - What impact will it have on your overall well-being?

3. **Take Action**: Choose the most practical solution and implement it.

   - What small steps will you take to ensure this solution works?
   - Reflect on the outcome and refine your approach as needed.

Inspirational Quotes and Reflections on Common-Sense

1. **"Common-sense is the collection of prejudices acquired by age 18."** – *Albert Einstein*

   - **Reflection**: Common-sense is often shaped by our experiences, upbringing, and culture. It's important to be open-minded and willing to challenge and expand our sense of what is common.

2. **"The only real wisdom is knowing you know nothing."** – *Socrates*

   - **Reflection**: True wisdom comes from humility and the recognition that we don't have all the answers. Common-sense allows us to remain open to new ideas and learn from our mistakes.

3. **"It is not enough to possess knowledge; one must also apply it."** – *Aristotle*

   - **Reflection**: Knowing something and putting it into practice are 2 very different things. Common-sense is about turning knowledge into actionable wisdom in our daily lives.

4. **"I have never met a man so ignorant that I couldn't learn something from him."** – *Galileo Galilei*

   - **Reflection**: Common-sense involves listening to others and learning from all situations, no matter how different they may be from our own perspective or expertise.

5. **"Do not go where the path may lead, go instead where there is no path and leave a trail."** – *Ralph Waldo Emerson*

   - **Reflection**: Common-sense isn't just about following convention; sometimes the most sensible thing is to pave your own way based on experience, instinct, and practical reasoning.

6. **"The greatest enemy of knowledge is not ignorance, it is the illusion of knowledge."** – *Stephen Hawking*

   - **Reflection**: Overconfidence can cloud our judgement. Common-sense reminds us to stay humble and seek out the truth through continuous learning and reflection.

7. **"In matters of style, swim with the current; in matters of principle, stand like a rock."** – *Thomas Jefferson*

   - **Reflection**: Common-sense teaches us to recognise when it's important to adapt and when to hold firm in our values, helping us navigate life with balance.

8. **"Common-sense is the most widely shared commodity in the world, for every man is convinced that he is well provided with it."** – *René Descartes*

   - **Reflection**: Often, we believe we possess all the common-sense we need. The key is recognising that true common-sense requires self-awareness and continual self-improvement.

9. **"Nothing in life is to be feared, it is only to be understood."** – *Marie Curie*

   - **Reflection**: Fear can cloud our judgement and hinder us from making practical decisions. Common-sense enables us to face challenges with a calm, rational approach based on understanding.

10. **"The more I learn, the more I realise how much I don't know."** – *Albert Einstein*

    - **Reflection**: True wisdom is understanding the limits of our knowledge and being open to learning. Common-sense helps us acknowledge our gaps and seek solutions in a practical manner.

11. **"The best way to predict the future is to create it."** – *Abraham Lincoln*

    - **Reflection**: Common-sense is not just about reacting to what happens around us, but proactively shaping our future with sound decisions and thoughtful actions.

12. **"What we know is a drop, what we don't know is an ocean."** – *Isaac Newton*

    - **Reflection**: This quote highlights the vastness of knowledge yet to be discovered. Common-sense reminds us to stay curious and humble, continuously learning and adapting.

13. **"It is not the strongest of the species that survive, nor the most intelligent, but the one most responsive to change."** – *Charles Darwin*

    - **Reflection**: Common-sense helps us recognise the importance of adaptability. The ability to respond to change with wisdom and flexibility is key to survival in both life and business.

14. **"The fool doth think he is wise, but the wise man knows himself to be a fool."** – *William Shakespeare*

   - **Reflection**: Humility is a hallmark of wisdom. Common-sense teaches us to recognise our limitations and continuously seek improvement.

15. **"A fool thinks himself to be wise, but a wise man knows himself to be a fool."** – *William Shakespeare*

   - **Reflection**: Wisdom comes from the realisation that no one has all the answers. Being aware of our own ignorance is part of exercising common-sense.

16. **"An ounce of practice is worth more than tonnes of preaching."** – *Mahatma Gandhi*

   - **Reflection**: Practical wisdom is best demonstrated through actions, not just words. Common-sense is about applying what we know in a real, tangible way to make a difference.

17. **"We are what we repeatedly do. Excellence, then, is not an act, but a habit."** – *Aristotle*

   - **Reflection**: Consistency in applying common-sense leads to excellence. It's through everyday practice that we shape our lives and decisions toward wisdom.

18. **"Success is not final, failure is not fatal: It is the courage to continue that counts."** – *Winston Churchill*

   - **Reflection**: Common-sense helps us persevere through both successes and failures. It's about maintaining resilience and practical judgement through every situation.

19. **"Do what you can, with what you have, where you are."** – *Theodore Roosevelt*

    - **Reflection**: This quote is about using the resources available to us and making the best decisions with what we know. It's the essence of common-sense practicality.

20. **"Success usually comes to those who are too busy to be looking for it."** – *Henry David Thoreau*

    - **Reflection**: Common-sense tells us that consistent effort and focus on our work often lead to success without the need for constant pursuit of accolades or recognition.

21. **"You miss 100% of the shots you don't take."** – *Wayne Gretzky*

    - **Reflection**: Common-sense encourages us to take calculated risks. If we hesitate or overthink, we miss out on opportunities. It's about acting with wisdom, even when the outcome is uncertain.

22. **"The function of wisdom is to discriminate between good and evil."** – *Cicero*

    - **Reflection**: Common-sense enables us to discern the right course of action in any given situation by relying on our judgement, experience, and moral compass.

23. **"Do not wait for leaders; do it alone, person to person."** – *Mother Teresa*

    - **Reflection**: Common-sense urges us to take responsibility for our actions, even in the absence of external direction or leadership.

24. **"Your task is not to seek for love, but merely to seek and find all the barriers within yourself that you have built against it."** – *Rumi*

   - **Reflection**: Common-sense in relationships is often about removing the barriers we create through fear or insecurity, allowing empathy and understanding to flourish.

25. **"The only thing necessary for the triumph of evil is for good men to do nothing."** – *Edmund Burke*

   - **Reflection**: Common-sense reminds us that standing up for what is right, even when it is difficult, is a fundamental part of leading a meaningful life.

26. **"The unexamined life is not worth living."** – *Socrates*

   - **Reflection**: Reflection is key to developing common-sense. By examining our choices, motivations, and actions, we can grow and make wiser decisions.

27. **"Everything should be made as simple as possible, but not simpler."** – *Albert Einstein*

   - **Reflection**: Common-sense often lies in simplifying complex issues without stripping away the essential truths. Simplicity leads to clarity.

28. **"Sometimes the questions are complicated and the answers are simple."** – *Dr. Seuss*

   - **Reflection**: Common-sense helps us identify straightforward solutions even in situations that initially appear complex or difficult.

29. **"The secret of getting ahead is getting started."** – *Mark Twain*

- **Reflection**: Procrastination often comes from overthinking. Common-sense teaches us to take small, practical steps to make progress instead of waiting for the perfect moment.

30. **"The most complicated skill is to be simple."** – *Dejan Stojanovic*

- **Reflection**: It takes wisdom to be able to strip away complexity and focus on what truly matters. Common-sense thrives in simplicity.

31. **"It is not how old you are, but how you are old."** – *Jules Renard*

- **Reflection**: Common-sense is not merely a product of age; it's the result of our willingness to reflect, adapt, and grow throughout our lives.

32. **"Life is what happens when you're busy making other plans."** – *John Lennon*

- **Reflection**: Sometimes, common-sense is about staying flexible and making the best decisions as life unfolds, rather than clinging to rigid plans.

33. **"In the middle of difficulty lies opportunity."** – *Albert Einstein*

- **Reflection**: Common-sense teaches us to see challenges as opportunities to grow, innovate, and make practical decisions that move us forward.

34. **"Success is not in what you have, but who you are."** – *Bo Bennett*

   - **Reflection**: Common-sense tells us that true success comes from our values, character, and decisions, rather than material wealth or superficial accomplishments.

35. **"In every walk with nature one receives far more than he seeks."** – *John Muir*

   - **Reflection**: Common-sense often encourages us to step outside of our routines and immerse ourselves in nature to find clarity and wisdom.

36. **"The best way to find yourself is to lose yourself in the service of others."** – *Mahatma Gandhi*

   - **Reflection**: Common-sense reminds us that true fulfilment comes not from selfish pursuits, but from helping others and being part of something greater than ourselves.

37. **"It's not whether you get knocked down, it's whether you get up."** – *Vince Lombardi*

   - **Reflection**: Life is full of setbacks, but common-sense teaches us that resilience and persistence are what truly lead to success and growth.

38. **"You have to learn the rules of the game. And then you have to play better than anyone else."** – *Albert Einstein*

   - **Reflection**: Common-sense encourages us to understand the rules, adapt, and improve. It's about mastering the fundamentals before striving for excellence.

39. **"The most important thing in life is to stop saying 'I wish' and start saying 'I will.'"** – *Charles Dickens*

- **Reflection**: Common-sense is about taking action. Saying "I will" reflects the practical mindset that turns aspirations into reality.

40. **"There are no shortcuts to any place worth going."** – *Beverly Sills*

- **Reflection**: True success requires hard work, persistence, and smart decisions. Common-sense tells us to avoid shortcuts and focus on sustainable growth.

41. **"To succeed in life, you need 2 things: ignorance and confidence."** – *Mark Twain*

- **Reflection**: Sometimes, not knowing the full scope of challenges ahead can help you move forward with courage. Confidence combined with common-sense can lead to success.

42. **"Don't cry because it's over, smile because it happened."** – *Dr. Seuss*

- **Reflection**: Common-sense teaches us to embrace both successes and failures as valuable learning experiences, cultivating a sense of gratitude rather than regret.

43. **"The harder I work, the luckier I get."** – *Samuel Goldwyn*

- **Reflection**: Luck is often a result of hard work, persistence, and good decision-making. Common-sense shows us that preparation often precedes success.

44. "Happiness depends upon ourselves." – *Aristotle*

- **Reflection**: Common-sense shows us that we have the power to shape our own happiness. External circumstances may influence us, but true contentment comes from within.

45. "Learn from yesterday, live for today, hope for tomorrow." – *Albert Einstein*

- **Reflection**: Common-sense teaches us to use our past experiences as lessons, embrace the present moment, and look forward to the future with optimism.

46. "A person who never made a mistake never tried anything new." – *Albert Einstein*

- **Reflection**: Common-sense encourages us to take risks and make mistakes. It's through trial and error that we grow and discover new opportunities.

47. "What lies behind us and what lies before us are tiny matters compared to what lies within us." – *Ralph Waldo Emerson*

- **Reflection**: Common-sense reminds us that our true strength comes from within. External factors can influence us, but our inner resolve guides our decisions and actions.

48. "Be yourself; everyone else is already taken." – *Oscar Wilde*

- **Reflection**: Common-sense encourages authenticity. The most successful decisions come from understanding who we are and acting in alignment with our true selves.

49. **"If you want to go fast, go alone. If you want to go far, go together."** – *African Proverb*

- **Reflection**: Collaboration and teamwork often lead to sustainable success. Common-sense teaches us the value of relationships and shared goals in achieving greater heights.

50. **"The only way to do great work is to love what you do."** – *Steve Jobs*

- **Reflection**: Common-sense reminds us that passion fuels excellence. It's not just about being smart, but about loving what you do enough to put in the effort to make it great.

51. **"A journey of a thousand miles begins with a single step."** – *Lao Tzu*

- **Reflection**: Common-sense teaches us that big achievements start with small, consistent actions. Don't wait for the perfect moment—take the first step.

52. **"The only thing we have to fear is fear itself."** – *Franklin D. Roosevelt*

- **Reflection**: Fear often holds us back. Common-sense encourages us to face our fears head-on and not let them control our actions or decisions.

53. **"Success is not final, failure is not fatal: It is the courage to continue that counts."** – *Winston Churchill*

- **Reflection**: True success comes from perseverance. Common-sense tells us that both success and failure are temporary, and what matters is our resilience.

54. **"The best time to plant a tree was 20 years ago. The second best time is now."** – *Chinese Proverb*

   - **Reflection**: Common-sense encourages us to act now, regardless of past opportunities. It's never too late to start working toward something important.

55. **"In the middle of every difficulty lies opportunity."** – *Albert Einstein*

   - **Reflection**: Challenges are often disguised opportunities. Common-sense helps us look beyond obstacles to see the lessons and growth they offer.

56. **"Success is how high you bounce when you hit bottom."** – *George S. Patton*

   - **Reflection**: It's not about avoiding failure but about how you respond to it. Common-sense tells us that resilience and attitude determine ultimate success.

57. **"Life is 10% what happens to us and 90% how we react to it."** – *Charles R. Swindoll*

   - **Reflection**: The way we respond to events shapes our reality. Common-sense teaches us to focus on our reactions rather than trying to control everything that happens.

58. **"Don't wait for the perfect moment. Take the moment and make it perfect."** – *Unknown*

   - **Reflection**: Common-sense encourages us to stop waiting for ideal conditions. The best time to act is now—create your own opportunities.

59. **"The only limit to our realisation of tomorrow is our doubts of today."** – *Franklin D. Roosevelt*

   - **Reflection**: Doubts often limit potential. Common-sense tells us that we can achieve anything if we overcome self-doubt and act confidently.

60. **"Life isn't about finding yourself. Life is about creating yourself."** – *George Bernard Shaw*

   - **Reflection**: Common-sense encourages us to actively shape our lives, rather than waiting for them to unfold on their own. We have the power to create our future.

61. **"Success usually comes to those who are too busy to be looking for it."** – *Henry David Thoreau*

   - **Reflection**: Focused work and dedication often lead to success. Common-sense suggests that success finds us when we're immersed in doing meaningful work.

62. **"The harder the battle, the sweeter the victory."** – *Les Brown*

   - **Reflection**: Tough challenges often lead to the most rewarding outcomes. Common-sense tells us that persistence and determination bring ultimate success.

63. **"Success is not the key to happiness. Happiness is the key to success."** – *Albert Schweitzer*

   - **Reflection**: True success comes from within. Common-sense teaches us that contentment and inner peace lead to real achievement, not the other way around.

64. **"The difference between who you are and who you want to be is what you do."** – *Unknown*

   - **Reflection**: Our actions define who we are. Common-sense tells us that to become the person we aspire to be, we must make choices aligned with that vision.

65. **"You don't have to be great to start, but you have to start to be great."** – *Zig Ziglar*

   - **Reflection**: Common-sense reminds us that greatness isn't instant. Starting is the key to progress, and improvement comes with time and effort.

66. **"It does not matter how slowly you go as long as you do not stop."** – *Confucius*

   - **Reflection**: Persistence is more important than speed. Common-sense teaches us that steady progress is key to long-term success.

67. **"Opportunities don't happen, you create them."** – *Chris Grosser*

   - **Reflection**: Common-sense shows us that success comes from proactive effort. We must take the initiative and create our own opportunities.

68. **"Success is the sum of small efforts, repeated day in and day out."** – *Robert Collier*

   - **Reflection**: Consistency is key. Common-sense teaches us that incremental efforts lead to significant outcomes over time.

69. **"The only way to do great work is to love what you do."** – *Steve Jobs*

- **Reflection**: Passion is the fuel for excellence. Common-sense shows us that loving our work makes the journey worthwhile and drives us to do our best.

70. **"Your time is limited, so don't waste it living someone else's life."** – *Steve Jobs*

- **Reflection**: Live authentically. Common-sense teaches us that our time is precious, and it's best spent pursuing our own passions, not imitating others.

71. **"It always seems impossible until it's done."** – *Nelson Mandela*

- **Reflection**: Common-sense tells us that impossible tasks become possible with determination and action. Nothing is too big to tackle.

72. **"Small daily improvements over time lead to stunning results."** – *Robin Sharma*

- **Reflection**: Small, consistent efforts lead to large improvements. Common-sense teaches us that long-term success comes from persistent action.

73. **"You miss 100% of the shots you don't take."** – *Wayne Gretzky*

- **Reflection**: Taking risks is necessary to succeed. Common-sense shows us that if we don't try, we can never succeed.

74. "To live a creative life, we must lose our fear of being wrong." – *Joseph Chilton Pearce*

- **Reflection**: Innovation requires risk. Common-sense teaches us that fear of failure limits creativity, and embracing mistakes leads to growth.

75. "What we think, we become." – *Buddha*

- **Reflection**: Our mindset shapes our reality. Common-sense shows us that positive thoughts lead to positive actions and outcomes.

76. "A goal without a plan is just a wish." – *Antoine de Saint-Exupery*

- **Reflection**: Goals require structure and direction. Common-sense teaches us that planning turns dreams into achievable outcomes.

77. "Success is not in what you have, but who you are." – *Bo Bennett*

- **Reflection**: True success is defined by our character and actions. Common-sense teaches us that inner qualities and values determine long-lasting success.

78. "The only way to do great work is to love what you do." – *Steve Jobs*

- **Reflection**: Passion drives success. Common-sense shows us that loving what we do enhances our chances of achieving greatness.

79. **"Life is what happens when you're busy making other plans."** – *John Lennon*

- **Reflection**: Common-sense teaches us that life is unpredictable. While planning is essential, it's also important to be flexible and enjoy the journey.

80. **"You must be the change you wish to see in the world."** – *Mahatma Gandhi*

- **Reflection**: Change starts from within. Common-sense reminds us that personal transformation leads to a broader impact on society.

81. **"The pessimist sees difficulty in every opportunity. The optimist sees opportunity in every difficulty."** – *Winston Churchill*

- **Reflection**: Perspective shapes success. Common-sense shows us that optimism allows us to find solutions, even in challenging situations.

82. **"Success is not the key to happiness. Happiness is the key to success."** – *Albert Schweitzer*

- **Reflection**: True fulfilment comes from happiness. Common-sense teaches us that joy in what we do is the secret to achieving success.

83. **"The future belongs to those who believe in the beauty of their dreams."** – *Eleanor Roosevelt*

- **Reflection**: Dream big, and believe in your abilities. Common-sense tells us that a clear vision combined with determination can turn dreams into reality.

84. **"The only limit to our realisation of tomorrow is our doubts of today."** – *Franklin D. Roosevelt*

- **Reflection**: Doubts hinder progress. Common-sense shows us that overcoming fear and believing in ourselves is key to realising our future potential.

85. **"Do not go where the path may lead, go instead where there is no path and leave a trail."** – *Ralph Waldo Emerson*

- **Reflection**: Common-sense encourages us to forge our own path. Innovation often comes from venturing into the unknown and creating new ways forward.

86. **"There are no limits to what you can accomplish, except the limits you place on your own thinking."** – *Brian Tracy*

- **Reflection**: Self-imposed boundaries limit potential. Common-sense teaches us to think beyond constraints and envision limitless possibilities.

87. **"The only thing standing between you and your goal is the story you keep telling yourself."** – *Jordan Belfort*

- **Reflection**: Our own narratives limit our success. Common-sense shows us that we can rewrite our stories to overcome barriers and achieve our goals.

88. **"We are what we repeatedly do. Excellence, then, is not an act, but a habit."** – *Aristotle*

- **Reflection**: Excellence is cultivated through consistent effort. Common-sense teaches us that habits shape outcomes, and greatness comes from daily dedication.

89. **"Strive not to be a success, but rather to be of value."** – *Albert Einstein*

- **Reflection**: Value is the foundation of success. Common-sense tells us that when we focus on serving others and adding value, success follows naturally.

90. **"The best way to predict the future is to create it."** – *Abraham Lincoln*

- **Reflection**: Common-sense encourages us to take control of our future. Instead of waiting for things to happen, we should create our own destiny.

91. **"The only impossible journey is the one you never begin."** – *Tony Robbins*

- **Reflection**: Starting is half the battle. Common-sense teaches us that the only way to achieve great things is by taking the first step, no matter how difficult it seems.

92. **"Success is not measured by what you accomplish, but by the obstacles you overcome."** – *Booker T. Washington*

- **Reflection**: Challenges define our growth. Common-sense shows us that the value of success lies in our ability to overcome adversity, not just in achieving goals.

93. **"Don't watch the clock; do what it does. Keep going."** – *Sam Levenson*

- **Reflection**: Patience and perseverance are keys to progress. Common-sense reminds us to keep moving forward, regardless of time constraints.

94. **"Don't let yesterday take up too much of today."** – *Will Rogers*

   - **Reflection**: Focus on the present. Common-sense tells us that past mistakes or successes should not hinder our current efforts; the present is where real work happens.

95. **"It always seems impossible until it's done."** – *Nelson Mandela*

   - **Reflection**: Persistence makes the impossible possible. Common-sense teaches us that challenges are temporary, and with effort, we can achieve the seemingly unachievable.

96. **"Believe you can and you're halfway there."** – *Theodore Roosevelt*

   - **Reflection**: Confidence is essential. Common-sense shows us that belief in oneself is the first step toward achieving success.

97. **"If you can dream it, you can do it."** – *Walt Disney*

   - **Reflection**: Dreams are the first step toward achievement. Common-sense teaches us that with hard work, any dream can become a reality.

98. **"In the end, we only regret the chances we didn't take."** – *Lewis Carroll*

   - **Reflection**: Opportunities are fleeting. Common-sense encourages us to take risks and seize chances when they present themselves.

99. **"It does not matter how slowly you go, as long as you do not stop."** – *Confucius*

   - **Reflection**: Perseverance is key. Common-sense teaches us that gradual progress is better than no progress at all.

100. **"Success is the sum of small efforts, repeated day in and day out."** – *Robert Collier*

- **Reflection**: Small actions lead to big results. Common-sense teaches us that consistency and effort, no matter how minor, compound into substantial success over time.

101. **"The best time to plant a tree was 20 years ago. The second best time is now."** – *Chinese Proverb*

- **Reflection**: It's never too late to start. Common-sense tells us that the present moment is the perfect time to take action.

102. **"Success is not the key to happiness. Happiness is the key to success."** – *Albert Schweitzer*

- **Reflection**: Fulfilment leads to achievement. Common-sense teaches us that when we prioritise happiness, success follows naturally.

103. **"Action is the foundational key to all success."** – *Pablo Picasso*

- **Reflection**: Success requires more than ideas; it demands action. Common-sense shows us that consistent effort is what drives results.

104. **"You miss 100% of the shots you don't take."** – *Wayne Gretzky*

- **Reflection**: Opportunities are only valuable when seized. Common-sense encourages us to take chances rather than miss out on potential success.

105. **"A person who never made a mistake never tried anything new."** – *Albert Einstein*

- **Reflection**: Mistakes are growth opportunities. Common-sense teaches us that innovation comes from taking risks and learning from failure.

106. **"You don't have to be great to start, but you have to start to be great."** – *Zig Ziglar*

- **Reflection**: Every journey begins with a single step. Common-sense shows us that greatness is born from the courage to begin.

107. **"Success usually comes to those who are too busy to be looking for it."** – *Henry David Thoreau*

- **Reflection**: Focus on your work, and success will find you. Common-sense tells us that dedication to the process brings results, not the pursuit of success itself.

108. **"The future belongs to those who believe in the beauty of their dreams."** – *Eleanor Roosevelt*

- **Reflection**: Believe in your potential. Common-sense teaches us that faith in our vision is the first step to turning dreams into reality.

109. **"It does not matter how slowly you go as long as you do not stop."** – *Confucius*

- **Reflection**: Persistence is paramount. Common-sense shows us that continuous progress, no matter the pace, leads to success.

110. **"The road to success and the road to failure are almost exactly the same."** – *Colin R. Davis*

- **Reflection**: Both paths require effort. Common-sense tells us that success and failure are simply results of choices and persistence.

111. **"Opportunities don't happen. You create them."** – *Chris Grosser*

- **Reflection**: You are the architect of your destiny. Common-sense shows us that successful people don't wait for opportunities—they create their own.

112. **"The only limit to our realisation of tomorrow is our doubts of today."** – *Franklin D. Roosevelt*

- **Reflection**: Doubts hold us back. Common-sense teaches us that self-belief is essential to unlock the future.

113. **"Success is not final, failure is not fatal: It is the courage to continue that counts."** – *Winston Churchill*

- **Reflection**: Resilience is key. Common-sense reminds us that both success and failure are temporary; persistence is what endures.

114. **"You don't have to be great to start, but you have to start to be great."** – *Zig Ziglar*

- **Reflection**: Starting is half the battle. Common-sense shows us that greatness comes from taking the first step, no matter how small.

115. **"The harder you work for something, the greater you'll feel when you achieve it."** – *Anonymous*

   - **Reflection**: Effort makes success sweeter. Common-sense tells us that the value of achievement is directly related to the work put into it.

116. **"Success is not in what you have, but who you are."** – *Bo Bennett*

   - **Reflection**: Character defines success. Common-sense shows us that true success is rooted in integrity and personal growth, not material wealth.

117. **"It always seems impossible until it's done."** – *Nelson Mandela*

   - **Reflection**: The impossible is just a challenge. Common-sense teaches us that perseverance turns seemingly impossible tasks into accomplishments.

118. **"Do not wait to strike till the iron is hot, but make it hot by striking."** – *William Butler Yeats*

   - **Reflection**: Create your opportunities. Common-sense shows us that action creates momentum and makes success possible.

119. **"Success is not measured by what you accomplish, but by the obstacles you overcome."** – *Booker T. Washington*

   - **Reflection**: Challenges are part of the journey. Common-sense teaches us that overcoming obstacles is a greater measure of success than the result itself.

120. **"If you want to achieve greatness stop asking for permission."** – *Anonymous*

- **Reflection**: Take ownership of your path. Common-sense encourages us to lead boldly, without seeking approval from others.

121. **"You cannot swim for new horizons until you have courage to lose sight of the shore."** – *William Faulkner*

- **Reflection**: Growth comes from stepping into the unknown. Common-sense tells us that only by letting go of the old can we reach new heights.

122. **"The way to get started is to quit talking and begin doing."** – *Walt Disney*

- **Reflection**: Action speaks louder than words. Common-sense shows us that success begins with doing, not just planning or talking.

123. **"What you get by achieving your goals is not as important as what you become by achieving your goals."** – *Zig Ziglar*

- **Reflection**: The journey shapes you. Common-sense teaches us that the process of striving toward goals is as important as the achievement itself.

124. **"Dream big and dare to fail."** – *Norman Vaughan*

- **Reflection**: Greatness requires boldness. Common-sense reminds us that we must take risks to achieve remarkable things.

125. **"It always seems impossible until it's done."** – *Nelson Mandela*

- **Reflection**: Obstacles are temporary. Common-sense shows us that perseverance and determination make what seems impossible achievable.

126. **"Don't let yesterday take up too much of today."** – *Will Rogers*

- **Reflection**: Focus on the present. Common-sense reminds us that past mistakes or successes should not hinder our current efforts; the present is where real work happens.

127. **"Success is not how high you have climbed, but how you make a positive difference to the world."** – *Roy T. Bennett*

- **Reflection**: Impact matters more than achievement. Common-sense shows us that the true measure of success is the positive difference we make in the lives of others.

128. **"You are never too old to set another goal or to dream a new dream."** – *C.S. Lewis*

- **Reflection**: It's never too late to start. Common-sense tells us that age is not a barrier to dreaming big and pursuing new goals.

129. **"The only way to do great work is to love what you do."** – *Steve Jobs*

- **Reflection**: Passion drives excellence. Common-sense teaches us that loving your work makes every challenge worth overcoming.

130. **"If you can dream it, you can do it."** – *Walt Disney*

   - **Reflection**: Vision is the first step. Common-sense shows us that with hard work, any dream can become a reality.

131. **"A goal without a plan is just a wish."** – *Antoine de Saint-Exupéry*

   - **Reflection**: Plans turn wishes into reality. Common-sense tells us that success comes from creating actionable steps toward our goals.

132. **"Success doesn't come from what you do occasionally, it comes from what you do consistently."** – *Marie Forleo*

   - **Reflection**: Consistency is key. Common-sense teaches us that small, consistent actions lead to big outcomes over time.

133. **"Everything you've ever wanted is on the other side of fear."** – *George Addair*

   - **Reflection**: Fear is the only obstacle. Common-sense shows us that overcoming fear is the key to unlocking the life we desire.

134. **"Start where you are. Use what you have. Do what you can."** – *Arthur Ashe*

   - **Reflection**: Begin with what you have. Common-sense teaches us that starting with limited resources is still better than waiting for the perfect moment.

135. **"Success is the sum of small efforts, repeated day in and day out."** – *Robert Collier*

   - **Reflection**: Success is built daily. Common-sense tells us that the cumulative effect of small efforts leads to great outcomes.

136. **"The secret of getting ahead is getting started."** – *Mark Twain*

   - **Reflection**: Action is the key to progress. Common-sense teaches us that the hardest part is often simply starting.

137. **"Life is 10% what happens to us and 90% how we react to it."** – *Charles R. Swindoll*

   - **Reflection**: Our response defines our journey. Common-sense reminds us that how we react to challenges shapes our success.

138. **"The best way to predict the future is to create it."** – *Abraham Lincoln*

   - **Reflection**: You are in control. Common-sense teaches us that by taking action today, we can shape tomorrow's outcomes.

139. **"Everything has beauty, but not everyone sees it."** – *Confucius*

   - **Reflection**: Perspective shapes reality. Common-sense tells us that beauty and opportunity are often hidden in plain sight, waiting for those who are willing to see.

140. **"Don't watch the clock; do what it does. Keep going."** – *Sam Levenson*

   - **Reflection**: Time is your ally. Common-sense teaches us that persistence, not impatience, brings success.

141. **"The future depends on what we do in the present."** – *Mahatma Gandhi*

   - **Reflection**: Now shapes tomorrow. Common-sense reminds us that the choices we make today will determine our future.

142. **"Your time is limited, so don't waste it living someone else's life."** – *Steve Jobs*

- **Reflection**: Own your path. Common-sense teaches us that the greatest fulfilment comes from living life on your terms.

143. **"Don't limit your challenges. Challenge your limits."** – *Anonymous*

- **Reflection**: Growth comes from pushing boundaries. Common-sense shows us that true progress is made when we test our limits and grow beyond them.

144. **"The only impossible journey is the one you never begin."** – *Tony Robbins*

- **Reflection**: Begin to make progress. Common-sense reminds us that the first step is often the most difficult but necessary for success.

145. **"The difference between who you are and who you want to be is what you do."** – *Anonymous*

- **Reflection**: Action defines identity. Common-sense teaches us that the path from where we are to where we want to be is paved by deliberate actions.

146. **"The key to success is to focus on goals, not obstacles."** – *Anonymous*

- **Reflection**: Focus drives achievement. Common-sense reminds us that a goal-focused mindset overcomes obstacles.

147. **"Success is how high you bounce when you hit bottom." –** *George S. Patton*

- **Reflection**: Resilience is a trait of success. Common-sense teaches us that setbacks are only temporary when we respond with resilience.

148. **"Our greatest glory is not in never falling, but in rising every time we fall." –** *Confucius*

- **Reflection**: Strength lies in recovery. Common-sense reminds us that falling down is inevitable, but rising again is what defines success.

149. **"Great things never come from comfort zones." –** *Anonymous*

- **Reflection**: Growth requires discomfort. Common-sense shows us that progress is made when we venture beyond the familiar.

150. **"The harder you work, the luckier you get." –** *Gary Player*

- **Reflection**: Luck favours the prepared. Common-sense teaches us that success is a result of hard work, not random chance.

Ankur and Vandana Quotes

151. "The more you trust your common-sense, the more you align with your true purpose."

- *Reflection*: Trusting your instincts and practical wisdom leads you closer to fulfilment.

152. "When the world becomes too complex, simplicity becomes the answer."

- *Reflection*: In the face of complexity, it's the simple solutions that often hold the most power.

153. "Wisdom isn't about knowing everything; it's about knowing what truly matters."

- *Reflection*: Wisdom lies in discerning what's important amidst all the noise.

154. "You don't have to have all the answers. You just need the courage to act with what you know."

- *Reflection*: Don't wait for certainty; move forward with what you know now.

155. **"Success is built on small, consistent actions that follow a clear path of common-sense."**

   - *Reflection*: Sustainable success comes from continuous effort, not just grand gestures.

156. **"The greatest leaders listen more than they speak, relying on their intuition and practical wisdom."**

   - *Reflection*: True leadership begins with understanding and using common-sense.

157. **"Common-sense is the foundation of innovation. It's not about reinventing the wheel, but making it work better."**

   - *Reflection*: Innovation thrives when it's rooted in practical understanding.

158. **"Simplicity is the ultimate sophistication."**

   - *Reflection*: The simpler the solution, the more powerful and elegant it becomes.

159. **"Every problem has a solution that lies in our ability to use common-sense."**

   - *Reflection*: The simplest solution is often the most effective when applied thoughtfully.

160. **"Don't overthink. Trust your instincts, and take the leap."**

   - *Reflection*: Overthinking paralyses progress. Trust yourself, and take action.

161. **"What you do today will shape your tomorrow—choose wisely."**

   - *Reflection*: Every action you take is a stepping stone toward your future.

162. **"The key to wisdom is not just learning; it's unlearning what no longer serves you."**

   - *Reflection*: Let go of outdated knowledge to make room for what truly helps you grow.

163. **"Success comes when you follow your common-sense, not the crowd."**

   - *Reflection*: Often, the path less travelled leads to the greatest rewards.

164. **"Trust your journey; it's designed for your unique growth."**

   - *Reflection*: Every experience is a part of your unique path—trust it.

165. **"Life doesn't have to be complicated. Let common-sense guide your decisions."**

   - *Reflection*: Life is simpler when we lean on practical wisdom to make choices.

166. **"The simplest idea can often solve the most complex problems."**

   - *Reflection*: Innovation isn't about complexity; it's about seeing the obvious solution in a new light.

167. **"Every day, your actions are writing your future story."**

   - *Reflection*: Every choice, no matter how small, shapes your tomorrow.

168. **"Action without clarity is like walking in the dark. Use common-sense to find your way."**

   - *Reflection*: Clarity comes when we make decisions rooted in common-sense, not confusion.

169. **"True strength lies in being adaptable and using practical wisdom to navigate challenges."**

   - *Reflection*: Flexibility and wisdom help you thrive in an ever-changing world.

170. **"The smartest people don't know everything; they know how to find what they need and act on it."**

   - *Reflection*: Wisdom is knowing how to navigate the unknown with confidence and clarity.

171. **"When in doubt, trust your common-sense—it's your inner compass."**

   - *Reflection*: Common-sense acts as a reliable guide when faced with uncertainty.

172. **"Success isn't just about ideas; it's about making those ideas happen with practical wisdom."**

   - *Reflection*: Common-sense turns ideas into action and action into success.

173. **"Life is simpler when we prioritise what matters most and let go of the rest."**

   - *Reflection*: Simplicity comes when we focus on the essentials and disregard distractions.

174. **"Every obstacle is an opportunity to apply common-sense and create a solution."**

   - *Reflection*: Challenges are stepping stones when we approach them with the right mindset.

175. "Wisdom is the ability to see what's important and make decisions based on that."

- *Reflection*: Clear vision and practical thinking bring clarity to any decision.

176. "The right decision isn't always the popular one—it's the one that makes the most sense."

- *Reflection*: Sometimes, doing what's right takes courage over conformity.

177. "Practical wisdom is your best tool for success—use it daily."

- *Reflection*: The more you use common-sense, the better you become at it.

178. "Simplicity is the secret to making a lasting impact."

- *Reflection*: Simplifying complex problems leads to lasting change.

179. "Common-sense is not a gift; it's a skill that can be developed."

- *Reflection*: Anyone can cultivate common-sense by practicing self-awareness and practical thinking.

180. "Every successful person follows a path of clear decisions, not complicated ones."

- *Reflection*: Success comes from clarity, focus, and simplicity in decision-making.

181. **"Empathy combined with common-sense makes the strongest leadership."**

   - *Reflection*: Leading with empathy and practical wisdom creates a path for sustainable success.

182. **"Great decisions are made by seeing the whole picture, not just the parts."**

   - *Reflection*: When you look beyond the immediate, you make choices that have long-term benefits.

183. **"The practical solution is always the one that moves you forward."**

   - *Reflection*: Inaction doesn't help; the right action, even small, is progress.

184. **"Simplicity isn't just a style, it's a way of life."**

   - *Reflection*: A simple life brings clarity, purpose, and peace.

185. **"Confidence comes not from knowing everything, but from trusting your ability to figure things out."**

   - *Reflection*: Confidence grows through problem-solving, not perfection.

186. **"True leaders understand that leadership is about guiding others with wisdom and humility."**

   - *Reflection*: Leadership isn't about authority, it's about empowering others with wisdom.

187. **"Success is never the result of one big decision, but a series of small, sensible choices."**

   - *Reflection*: Every successful journey is made up of a thousand small decisions that add up over time.

188. **"To achieve greatness, you need to think simply and act wisely."**

- *Reflection*: Simple thinking and wise action create the foundation for extraordinary achievements.

189. **"No matter how complex the challenge, the right answer is always rooted in simplicity."**

- *Reflection*: Simple solutions are often the most effective and sustainable.

190. **"The best decisions come when logic and common-sense align."**

- *Reflection*: When reason and practicality come together, the best outcomes follow.

191. **"The only way to navigate life's complexity is with clarity, confidence, and common-sense."**

- *Reflection*: A clear mind and practical approach help you deal with anything that comes your way.

192. **"Great leaders aren't born; they're made by the wise decisions they consistently make."**

- *Reflection*: Leadership is shaped by the actions you take, not titles you hold.

193. **"It's not about having all the answers, it's about making the best decisions with the information at hand."**

- *Reflection*: Success comes from acting wisely with the knowledge you have, not from knowing everything.

194. "Wisdom is knowing when to act and when to wait."

- *Reflection*: Timing is everything; knowing when to act is just as important as knowing how.

195. "Your success is determined by the clarity of your choices and the simplicity of your actions."

- *Reflection*: The clearer your goals and the simpler your steps, the closer you come to success.

196. "Common-sense is the bridge between what we know and what we need to do."

- *Reflection*: It's the link between knowledge and effective action.

197. "Clarity and simplicity in decision-making will always win over complexity."

- *Reflection*: Clear, straightforward choices lead to better outcomes.

198. "In every challenge, there's a simple solution waiting to be discovered."

- *Reflection*: Common-sense uncovers the solutions we often overlook in the face of complexity.

199. "Success isn't about knowing everything; it's about knowing what to focus on."

- *Reflection*: Focus your energy on the important and let go of distractions.

200. "Leadership without wisdom is like a ship without a rudder."

- *Reflection*: Wisdom is the guiding force behind great leadership and lasting impact.

Appendix 5

Examples of Common-Sense Practices for Staying Healthy

Maintaining good health requires a combination of daily habits and a balanced lifestyle. Common-sense health practices focus on simple, effective, and sustainable actions that support overall well-being. Here are examples of common-sense practices for health:

1. **Eating a Balanced Diet:**

   - **Practice**: Consume a variety of fruits, vegetables, lean proteins, whole grains, and healthy fats to ensure your body gets the essential nutrients it needs.

   - **Common-sense**: A well-rounded diet supports energy levels, immune function, and overall health, while reducing the risk of chronic diseases.

2. **Staying Hydrated:**

   - **Practice**: Drink plenty of water throughout the day to maintain hydration and support bodily functions.

   - **Common-sense**: Proper hydration is essential for digestion, circulation, temperature regulation, and toxin removal, making it vital for overall health.

3. Getting Regular Exercise:

- **Practice**: Engage in regular physical activity, such as walking, running, swimming, or yoga, to keep your body strong and fit.

- **Common-sense**: Exercise promotes cardiovascular health, strengthens muscles, boosts energy, and improves mental well-being.

4. Prioritising Sleep:

- **Practice**: Aim for 7-9 hours of quality sleep each night to allow your body to recover, repair, and regenerate.

- **Common-sense**: Consistent, restful sleep is crucial for cognitive function, mood regulation, immune health, and overall vitality.

5. Managing Stress:

- **Practice**: Incorporate stress-management techniques such as deep breathing, meditation, mindfulness, or hobbies that help you relax and unwind.

- **Common-sense**: Chronic stress can negatively impact physical and mental health. Managing stress effectively is essential for maintaining a balanced, healthy life.

6. Maintaining Healthy Weight:

- **Practice**: Achieve and maintain a healthy weight by balancing calorie intake with physical activity.

- **Common-sense**: Maintaining a healthy weight helps prevent conditions like heart disease, diabetes, and joint problems, contributing to a longer and healthier life.

7. Avoiding Smoking and Excessive Alcohol:

- **Practice**: Refrain from smoking and limit alcohol consumption to moderate levels to reduce the risk of serious health problems.

- **Common-sense**: Both smoking and excessive alcohol consumption are linked to various health issues, including respiratory, cardiovascular, and liver diseases.

8. Practicing Good Hygiene:

- **Practice**: Wash hands regularly, brush and floss teeth daily, and maintain cleanliness to prevent infections and illnesses.

- **Common-sense**: Good hygiene reduces the risk of bacteria, viruses, and other pathogens, helping to prevent illness and promote overall health.

9. Taking Regular Breaks:

- **Practice**: Take short breaks throughout the day to move around, stretch, and rest your eyes, especially if you're working or studying for long periods.

- **Common-sense**: Taking breaks helps reduce fatigue, prevents muscle strain, and improves productivity while maintaining physical and mental well-being.

10. Building Strong Social Connections:

- **Practice**: Maintain positive relationships with family, friends, and community to promote emotional and mental health.

- **Common-sense**: Social interactions improve mood, reduce stress, and contribute to mental resilience, making them vital for a healthy and fulfilling life.

11. Preventive Healthcare:

- **Practice**: Schedule regular health check-ups, screenings, and vaccinations to catch potential health issues early and maintain your well-being.

- **Common-sense**: Preventive care helps identify risks and address them before they become serious problems, leading to better long-term health outcomes.

12. Limiting Screen Time:

- **Practice**: Reduce the amount of time spent on digital devices to avoid eye strain, poor posture, and mental fatigue.

- **Common-sense**: Limiting screen time helps prevent physical discomfort (such as eye strain and headaches) and promotes better sleep and mental health.

13. Listening to Your Body:

- **Practice**: Pay attention to signs of fatigue, discomfort, or illness, and take appropriate action to address them.

- **Common-sense**: Listening to your body helps prevent overexertion and enables early detection of potential health issues, promoting long-term well-being.

14. Practice Moderation:

- **Practice**: Avoid extreme diets, excessive exercise, or overindulgence in unhealthy habits. Moderation is key to a balanced lifestyle.

- **Common-sense**: Finding balance in all aspects of life, from eating to exercising, helps maintain sustainable health without unnecessary strain on the body.

15. **Engaging in Mental Health Care:**

- **Practice**: Take time to care for your mental health through practices like journaling, therapy, or simply relaxing in nature.

- **Common-sense**: Mental well-being is just as important as physical health, and caring for your mental health supports overall emotional resilience and physical health.

These common-sense health practices help you build a strong foundation for physical, mental, and emotional well-being, leading to a healthier and more fulfilling life.

Examples of Common-Sense for Shifting from Limiting Mindset to Empowering Mindset

Shifting from a limiting mindset to an empowering mindset involves adopting positive and constructive perspectives to overcome challenges and pursue personal growth. Here are examples of common-sense approaches for making this shift:

1. **Believing in Growth:**

   - **Limiting Mindset**: "I'm not good at this, and I never will be."

   - **Empowering Mindset**: "I may not be good at this yet, but with effort and learning, I can improve."

   - **Common-sense**: Embracing the belief that abilities can be developed with dedication and learning is common-sense for fostering a growth mindset.

2. **Focusing on Solutions:**

   - **Limiting Mindset**: "This problem is too big; there's nothing I can do."

- **Empowering Mindset**: "I can't change everything, but I can focus on what I can control and find solutions."

- **Common-sense**: Directing energy toward finding solutions rather than dwelling on problems is common-sense for empowerment.

3. Learning from Failure:

- **Limiting Mindset**: "I failed, and that means I'm not capable."

- **Empowering Mindset**: "Failure is an opportunity to learn and grow; it doesn't define my capabilities."

- **Common-sense**: Recognising that failure is a natural part of the learning process and an opportunity for improvement is common-sense for an empowering mindset.

4. Embracing Challenges:

- **Limiting Mindset**: "I avoid challenges because they might expose my weaknesses."

- **Empowering Mindset**: "Challenges help me grow, and I'm capable of overcoming them."

- **Common-sense**: Embracing challenges as opportunities for personal development and learning is common-sense for cultivating an empowering mindset.

5. Cultivating Positive Self-Talk:

- **Limiting Mindset**: "I'm not good enough; I'll never succeed."

- **Empowering Mindset**: "I am capable, and I believe in my ability to overcome obstacles."

- **Common-sense**: Using positive self-talk to reinforce a belief in one's abilities and potential is common-sense for an empowering mindset.

6. Setting Realistic Goals:

- **Limiting Mindset**: "I can't achieve big goals; they're too unrealistic."

- **Empowering Mindset**: "I can break down big goals into smaller, achievable steps."

- **Common-sense**: Setting realistic and achievable goals while recognising the power of incremental progress is common-sense for empowerment.

7. Seeking Continuous Learning:

- **Limiting Mindset**: "I already know enough; there's nothing more to learn."

- **Empowering Mindset**: "There's always room for growth and learning in every aspect of life."

- **Common-sense**: Acknowledging that learning is a lifelong process and seeking opportunities for continuous improvement is common-sense for an empowering mindset.

8. Surrounding Oneself with Positivity:

- **Limiting Mindset**: "Negative people and situations always bring me down."

- **Empowering Mindset**: "I choose to surround myself with positivity and uplifting influences."

- **Common-sense**: Recognising the impact of one's environment on mindset and actively choosing positive influences is common-sense for empowerment.

9. Expressing Gratitude:

- **Limiting Mindset**: "I focus on what's lacking in my life."

- **Empowering Mindset**: "I express gratitude for what I have, fostering a positive perspective."

- **Common-sense**: Acknowledging and appreciating the positive aspects of life contributes to an empowering mindset.

10. Taking Initiative:

- **Limiting Mindset**: "I wait for things to happen; I have no control."

- **Empowering Mindset**: "I take initiative and actively shape my life and choices."

- **Common-sense**: Recognising the power of personal agency and taking proactive steps toward goals is common-sense for empowerment.

11. Celebrating Successes:

- **Limiting Mindset**: "I downplay my achievements; they're not that significant."

- **Empowering Mindset**: "I celebrate my successes, no matter how small, and acknowledge my growth."

- **Common-sense**: Celebrating achievements, no matter how minor, reinforces a positive mindset and fosters empowerment.

12. Being Open to Change:

- **Limiting Mindset**: "I fear change because it disrupts my comfort zone."

- **Empowering Mindset**: "Change brings opportunities for growth and new experiences."

- **Common-sense**: Acknowledging that change is a natural part of life and an opportunity for growth is common-sense for fostering an empowering mindset.

These examples demonstrate how common-sense approaches can help shift from a limiting mindset to an empowering mindset by embracing positivity, resilience, and a belief in one's ability to overcome challenges.

Examples of Common-Sense Practices for Intellectual Growth

Intellectual growth is essential for personal and professional development. It involves expanding one's knowledge, improving critical thinking skills, and cultivating a curious mindset. Here are examples of common-sense practices to promote intellectual growth:

1. **Reading Regularly:**

   - **Practice**: Reading books, articles, and other materials regularly exposes you to new ideas, perspectives, and knowledge.

   - **Common-sense**: Constant exposure to diverse content is one of the most effective ways to stimulate intellectual growth and broaden your horizons.

2. **Asking Questions:**

   - **Practice**: Cultivating a habit of asking questions allows you to dig deeper into topics, challenge assumptions, and understand concepts more thoroughly.

- **Common-sense**: Intellectual growth often begins with curiosity. By asking thoughtful questions, you push yourself to explore and learn beyond surface-level knowledge.

3. Engaging in Meaningful Conversations:

- **Practice**: Engaging with people who have different viewpoints and expertise challenges your thinking and introduces new concepts.

- **Common-sense**: Healthy debates and discussions help refine your ideas, sharpen your reasoning skills, and encourage intellectual flexibility.

4. Seeking Feedback and Constructive Criticism:

- **Practice**: Actively seeking feedback from others allows you to identify areas of improvement and grow intellectually.

- **Common-sense**: Embracing feedback helps you correct mistakes, refine ideas, and expand your understanding, ultimately enhancing your intellectual capacity.

5. Staying Open-Minded:

- **Practice**: Keeping an open mind means being willing to consider new information and revise previously held beliefs based on evidence or new experiences.

- **Common-sense**: Being open to change and new ideas is crucial for intellectual growth, as it allows you to adapt and learn continuously.

6. Critical Thinking and Reflection:

- **Practice**: Regularly reflecting on your thoughts, decisions, and actions, while practicing critical thinking, helps you process information deeply and make informed judgements.

- **Common-sense**: Taking time to critically assess ideas and experiences encourages intellectual development by allowing you to refine your thought process and avoid cognitive biases.

7. Setting Learning Goals:

- **Practice**: Setting specific, measurable, and achievable learning goals keeps you focused on your intellectual growth and ensures you make progress.

- **Common-sense**: Goal-setting aligns your efforts and helps maintain motivation, ultimately leading to sustained intellectual development.

8. Maintaining a Growth Mindset:

- **Practice**: Believing that intelligence and abilities can be developed through hard work and dedication fosters continuous improvement.

- **Common-sense**: A growth mindset encourages resilience, perseverance, and a commitment to lifelong learning, all of which are key to intellectual growth.

9. Exploring New Interests:

- **Practice**: Dipping into areas outside your usual interests and comfort zone exposes you to diverse knowledge and skills.

- **Common-sense**: Intellectual growth thrives when you challenge yourself to explore topics that are unfamiliar or different from your expertise.

10. Practicing Mindful Learning:

- **Practice**: Being fully present and engaged while learning, whether through focused study sessions or hands-on practice, enhances retention and understanding.

- **Common-sense**: Mindful learning ensures that you absorb knowledge effectively, as it encourages deeper attention and a more intentional learning process.

11. Using Technology to Enhance Learning:

- **Practice**: Leveraging digital tools, online courses, podcasts, and educational apps to access diverse resources allows you to learn efficiently.

- **Common-sense**: Technology provides an abundance of knowledge at your fingertips, making it a valuable tool for continuous intellectual development.

12. Journaling for Clarity:

- **Practice**: Writing down thoughts, ideas, and reflections helps clarify understanding and improves cognitive processing.

- **Common-sense**: Journaling fosters deeper thinking by allowing you to organise and articulate ideas, which leads to enhanced comprehension and intellectual growth.

By adopting these common-sense practices, individuals can cultivate intellectual growth, expand their perspectives, and become more effective learners. These habits contribute to a lifelong journey of continuous improvement and intellectual enrichment.

Examples of Common-Sense Practices for Emotional Well-Being

Maintaining emotional well-being is essential for a balanced and fulfilling life. Common-sense practices for emotional health focus on building resilience, managing stress, and nurturing positive relationships. Here are 10 examples of common-sense practices for emotional well-being:

1. **Practicing Gratitude:**

   - **Practice**: Take a moment each day to reflect on things you're grateful for, big or small.

   - **Common-sense**: Gratitude shifts focus from what's lacking to what's abundant, fostering a positive outlook and emotional resilience.

2. **Expressing Emotions:**

   - **Practice**: Allow yourself to express your emotions, whether through talking, journaling, or creative outlets like art or music.

   - **Common-sense**: Suppressing emotions can lead to stress and emotional discomfort. Healthy expression helps release built-up tension and fosters emotional clarity.

3. Building Strong Relationships:

- **Practice**: Nurture positive, supportive relationships with family, friends, and peers.

- **Common-sense**: Strong connections provide emotional support, reduce stress, and improve overall mental health.

4. Setting Healthy Boundaries:

- **Practice**: Learn to say no when necessary and protect your time and energy from undue stress or obligations.

- **Common-sense**: Setting boundaries ensures that you can protect your emotional well-being without feeling overwhelmed or drained.

5. Engaging in Self-Care:

- **Practice**: Take regular breaks for activities that replenish your energy, such as taking a walk, reading, or enjoying a hobby.

- **Common-sense**: Self-care is essential for maintaining emotional balance and prevents burnout, ensuring that you can recharge both mentally and emotionally.

6. Practicing Mindfulness:

- **Practice**: Engage in mindfulness or meditation practices to stay grounded in the present moment and reduce emotional stress.

- **Common-sense**: Mindfulness helps reduce overthinking, lowers anxiety, and cultivates emotional calmness by focusing on the present instead of worrying about the past or future.

7. Seeking Help When Needed:

- **Practice**: Don't hesitate to seek professional help or talk to someone you trust when you're feeling overwhelmed.

- **Common-sense**: Asking for support is a sign of strength, not weakness. It helps you process emotions and gain a fresh perspective on challenging situations.

8. Accepting Imperfection:

- **Practice**: Embrace your imperfections and practice self-compassion instead of being overly critical of yourself.

- **Common-sense**: Self-acceptance fosters emotional well-being, reducing feelings of inadequacy and allowing you to embrace life's ups and downs with resilience.

9. Engaging in Positive Self-Talk:

- **Practice**: Replace negative thoughts with kind and constructive affirmations that support your emotional health.

- **Common-sense**: Positive self-talk boosts self-esteem, reduces anxiety, and empowers you to handle challenges with confidence and calmness.

10. Managing Stress Effectively:

- **Practice**: Develop effective coping strategies for stress, such as physical exercise, relaxation techniques, or taking time out to decompress.

- **Common-sense**: Managing stress is vital for emotional well-being. Having a toolbox of stress-relief practices helps maintain emotional stability during difficult times.

By incorporating these common-sense practices into your daily routine, you can enhance your emotional well-being, build resilience, and develop a more balanced, fulfilling life.

Examples of Common-Sense Practices for Financial Hygiene

1. **Create a Budget:**

   - **Common-sense**: Track your income and expenses to create a budget. Understanding where your money goes allows you to make informed decisions, control spending, and save more.

2. **Save Regularly:**

   - **Common-sense**: Set aside a portion of your income for savings. Whether it's for an emergency fund, retirement, or future goals, saving regularly helps ensure financial security.

3. **Live Within Your Means:**

   - **Common-sense**: Avoid spending more than you earn. Stick to your budget, prioritise essentials, and limit unnecessary expenses to prevent accumulating debt.

4. **Pay Off Debt:**

   - **Common-sense**: If you have debt, create a plan to pay it off. Focus on high-interest debts first, and try to avoid accumulating new debt while reducing existing liabilities.

5. Build an Emergency Fund:

- **Common-sense**: Aim to save at least 3 to 6 months' worth of living expenses in an easily accessible account for unexpected situations like medical emergencies, job loss, or urgent repairs.

6. Invest for the Future:

- **Common-sense**: Start investing early to build wealth over time. Whether it's through stocks, bonds, or retirement accounts, investing allows your money to grow and work for you.

7. Monitor Your Credit Score:

- **Common-sense**: Regularly check your credit score to ensure there are no errors or fraud. A good credit score helps you secure loans at favourable interest rates.

8. Avoid Impulse Purchases:

- **Common-sense**: Before making a purchase, take a moment to assess whether it's necessary. Impulse buying can quickly lead to unnecessary expenses and financial strain.

9. Review Financial Goals Regularly:

- **Common-sense**: Assess your financial goals periodically and make adjustments as needed. Life changes, and so do your priorities, so regularly reviewing your goals ensures you stay on track.

10. Protect Your Finances with Insurance:

- **Common-sense**: Safeguard your financial well-being by getting adequate insurance coverage, such as health, life, auto, and home insurance. It provides protection against unexpected financial burdens.

By following these common-sense financial practices, you can maintain good financial hygiene, ensure financial stability, and work towards achieving your financial goals.

Examples of Common-Sense in Personal Relationships with Family, Friends, and Relatives

---

History, when illuminated by the light of common-sense, becomes a guidebook for navigating the challenges of the present
– Vandana

Healthy personal relationships require empathy, respect, understanding, and open communication. Here are examples of common-sense practices to foster better relationships with family, friends, and relatives:

1. **Active Listening:**

   - **Practice**: When someone shares their thoughts or concerns, listen attentively without interrupting.

   - **Common-sense**: Listening with empathy helps you understand others' perspectives and strengthens trust and connection in relationships.

2. Being Present:

- **Practice**: Make time to be fully present when spending time with loved ones, without distractions like phones or work.

- **Common-sense**: Being emotionally and physically available enhances the quality of your interactions and shows your commitment to the relationship.

3. Expressing Appreciation:

- **Practice**: Regularly express gratitude and appreciation for the people in your life.

- **Common-sense**: Acknowledging others' contributions, big or small, fosters goodwill and reinforces positive feelings within relationships.

4. Respecting Boundaries:

- **Practice**: Understand and respect personal boundaries in your relationships, whether it's physical space, emotional needs, or time limits.

- **Common-sense**: Respecting boundaries promotes mutual understanding, trust, and prevents feelings of being overwhelmed or disrespected.

5. Offering Support During Tough Times:

- **Practice**: Be there for family and friends when they are going through difficulties, offering support without being asked.

- **Common-sense**: Offering help during challenging times shows you care and strengthens emotional bonds.

6. Being Honest and Transparent:

- **Practice**: Share your thoughts and feelings openly and honestly with those close to you.

- **Common-sense**: Open communication builds trust and ensures everyone is on the same page, avoiding misunderstandings and fostering deeper connections.

7. Forgiving and Letting Go of Grudges:

- **Practice**: When conflicts arise, approach forgiveness with an open heart and be willing to let go of past grievances.

- **Common-sense**: Holding onto grudges only harms relationships. Forgiveness is key to maintaining peace and moving forward in a healthy way.

8. Showing Empathy:

- **Practice**: Understand and acknowledge others' emotions, showing that you care about their feelings and struggles.

- **Common-sense**: Empathy strengthens emotional connections and builds a foundation of trust and mutual respect.

9. Setting Time Aside for Family and Friends:

- **Practice**: Prioritise spending quality time with loved ones, whether it's through regular visits, phone calls, or fun activities.

- **Common-sense**: Regularly investing time in your relationships helps them grow and strengthens your bond with others.

10. **Respecting Differences:**

- **Practice**: Accept and respect the differences in personality, opinion, or lifestyle that each individual brings to the relationship.

- **Common-sense**: Acknowledging that everyone is unique and has their own perspectives promotes harmony and mutual respect.

11. **Being Patient:**

- **Practice**: Practice patience during misunderstandings or disagreements and take time to work through them constructively.

- **Common-sense**: Patience allows for calmer, more thoughtful responses and prevents escalating tensions during difficult conversations.

12. **Offering Apologies When Necessary:**

- **Practice**: When you make a mistake, apologise sincerely and take responsibility for your actions.

- **Common-sense**: Apologising when wrong shows humility and respect for others' feelings, helping to rebuild trust and harmony.

13. **Celebrating Milestones Together:**

- **Practice**: Take part in important events, such as birthdays, achievements, or anniversaries, to show that you care about the person's happiness.

- **Common-sense**: Celebrating milestones creates positive memories and reinforces your emotional connection with family and friends.

14. **Balancing Independence and Togetherness:**

- **Practice**: Respect each other's need for personal space while also ensuring there's time for shared experiences.

- **Common-sense**: Striking a balance between personal independence and mutual time together allows for healthier, more respectful relationships.

15. **Being Supportive in Growth and Change:**

- **Practice**: Encourage personal growth and support the changes your loved ones go through, whether in career, lifestyle, or self-development.

- **Common-sense**: Supporting others during their growth journey fosters an environment of trust, encouragement, and love.

These common-sense practices serve as the foundation for building and maintaining strong, healthy relationships with family, friends, and relatives. By treating others with kindness, respect, and empathy, you nurture a positive environment for growth, connection, and long-lasting bonds.

Examples of Common-Sense Practices for Relationship with Self

Examples of Common-Sense Practices for a Relationship with Self:

1. **Prioritise Self-Care:**

   - **Common-sense**: Rest, hydrate, eat nutritious food, and exercise regularly to maintain physical and mental well-being.

2. **Practice Self-Compassion:**

   - **Common-sense**: Be kind to yourself during failures or setbacks instead of being overly critical.

3. **Set Healthy Boundaries:**

   - **Common-sense**: Recognise your limits and say "no" when necessary to protect your time and energy.

4. **Invest in Personal Growth:**

   - **Common-sense**: Read, learn new skills, or pursue hobbies to continuously develop and enrich your life.

5. Acknowledge Your Strengths:

- **Common-sense**: Regularly remind yourself of your achievements and unique qualities to build self-confidence.

6. Listen to Your Body and Mind:

- **Common-sense**: Pay attention to signs of stress, fatigue, or discomfort, and take action to address them.

7. Cultivate Gratitude:

- **Common-sense**: Reflect on things you appreciate about yourself and your life to foster positivity.

8. Take Responsibility for Choices:

- **Common-sense**: Own up to mistakes and learn from them, instead of blaming others or external circumstances.

9. Engage in Mindful Practices:

- **Common-sense**: Meditate, journal, or practice mindfulness to stay present and reduce unnecessary stress.

10. Celebrate Your Individuality:

- **Common-sense**: Accept who you are, embrace your quirks, and live authentically rather than comparing yourself to others.

These practices reinforce a healthy, empowering relationship with yourself, laying the foundation for a balanced and fulfilling life.

Examples of Common-Sense Practices in Marital Relationships

A healthy marital relationship is built on love, respect, communication, and mutual understanding. Here are examples of common-sense practices to nurture a strong and fulfilling marriage:

1. **Effective Communication:**

   - **Practice**: Share thoughts, feelings, and concerns openly with your spouse, and listen attentively when they speak.

   - **Common-sense**: Clear communication fosters mutual understanding, helps resolve conflicts, and prevents misunderstandings in the relationship.

2. **Showing Appreciation:**

   - **Practice**: Regularly express gratitude for the things your spouse does, whether big or small.

   - **Common-sense**: Showing appreciation strengthens emotional bonds and makes your spouse feel valued and loved.

3. Respecting Each Other's Space:

- **Practice**: Recognise and respect your spouse's need for personal time or space.

- **Common-sense**: Giving each other room to grow individually prevents feelings of suffocation and supports healthy interdependence.

4. Compromising and Finding Common Ground:

- **Practice**: Understand that disagreements are a part of any relationship, and find ways to compromise and meet halfway.

- **Common-sense**: Compromise is essential for maintaining harmony in the relationship and finding solutions that work for both partners.

5. Being Supportive in Each Other's Goals:

- **Practice**: Encourage your spouse in their personal and professional aspirations and support them in their endeavours.

- **Common-sense**: Supporting each other's dreams helps build a strong partnership based on mutual respect and encouragement.

6. Prioritising Quality Time Together:

- **Practice**: Set aside time for regular date nights or shared activities to nurture your bond.

- **Common-sense**: Spending quality time together strengthens emotional intimacy and keeps the relationship fresh and vibrant.

7. Handling Conflict Calmly:

- **Practice**: When disagreements arise, approach them calmly, focusing on solving the issue, not attacking each other.

- **Common-sense**: Handling conflict with respect and maturity reduces tension and fosters healthier, more productive conversations.

8. Being Honest and Transparent:

- **Practice**: Be open about your feelings, needs, and concerns, and encourage your spouse to do the same.

- **Common-sense**: Honesty builds trust, and transparency strengthens the foundation of any relationship.

9. Forgiving and Letting Go of Grudges:

- **Practice**: Practice forgiveness when your spouse makes a mistake, and avoid holding onto past wrongs.

- **Common-sense**: Letting go of grudges prevents bitterness and helps both partners move forward with a clean slate.

10. Sharing Responsibilities:

- **Practice**: Share household chores, financial responsibilities, and parenting duties equally or in a way that feels fair to both partners.

- **Common-sense**: A balanced division of responsibilities prevents resentment and promotes teamwork within the marriage.

11. Supporting Each Other's Emotional Needs:

- **Practice**: Offer emotional support and be there for each other during difficult times.

- **Common-sense**: Being emotionally available strengthens the emotional connection between spouses and builds trust and safety in the relationship.

12. Maintaining Physical Intimacy:

- **Practice**: Regular physical affection, such as holding hands, hugging, or kissing, helps maintain closeness.

- **Common-sense**: Physical intimacy is an important part of marital connection and emotional bonding.

13. Celebrating Special Occasions:

- **Practice**: Celebrate anniversaries, birthdays, and other significant events together to show love and appreciation.

- **Common-sense**: Recognising milestones in the relationship helps keep the marriage strong and reminds both partners of the value of their bond.

14. Being Patient with Each Other:

- **Practice**: Be patient and understanding during stressful or challenging times, and give each other space to process emotions.

- **Common-sense**: Patience is crucial in preventing conflicts from escalating and allows both partners to approach problems with calmness and empathy.

15. Maintaining a Sense of Humour:

- **Practice**: Don't take everything too seriously. Find moments to laugh together and enjoy each other's company.

- **Common-sense**: Humour lightens the mood, strengthens emotional bonds, and helps couples navigate challenges with a positive attitude.

16. Checking In Regularly:

- **Practice**: Regularly check-in with each other about how things are going in the marriage and express needs or concerns.

- **Common-sense**: Frequent communication ensures that both partners feel heard and can address any issues before they become problems.

These common-sense practices can help couples create a strong, loving, and respectful marriage. By being kind, empathetic, communicative, and supportive, partners can navigate life's ups and downs together while maintaining a healthy and thriving relationship.

Examples of Common-Sense Practices in Parenting

Parenting is a dynamic and evolving experience, and common-sense practices can significantly enhance the parent-child relationship and promote healthy development. Here are examples of common-sense parenting strategies:

1. **Setting Clear Boundaries:**

   - **Practice**: Establish clear, consistent rules and expectations for behaviour.

   - **Common-sense**: Boundaries help children understand limits, providing a sense of security and teaching them responsibility.

2. **Modelling Desired Behaviour:**

   - **Practice**: Demonstrate the values and behaviours you want to see in your child (e.g., kindness, patience, respect).

   - **Common-sense**: Children often imitate their parents, so modelling positive behaviour encourages them to follow suit.

3. Listening Actively to Your Child:

- **Practice**: Listen to your child's concerns, feelings, and thoughts without interruption or judgement.

- **Common-sense**: Active listening fosters trust, strengthens the parent-child relationship, and shows the child that their voice matters.

4. Providing Positive Reinforcement:

- **Practice**: Recognise and praise your child's good behaviour and achievements.

- **Common-sense**: Positive reinforcement boosts self-esteem, encourages continued good behaviour, and helps children feel valued.

5. Being Consistent with Discipline:

- **Practice**: Respond to misbehaviour consistently, using appropriate consequences that are fair and understandable.

- **Common-sense**: Consistency in discipline helps children understand the connection between actions and consequences, promoting responsible behaviour.

6. Encouraging Independence:

- **Practice**: Allow your child to make age-appropriate decisions and take on responsibilities.

- **Common-sense**: Encouraging independence helps children develop confidence, problem-solving skills, and a sense of ownership over their actions.

7. Balancing Structure with Flexibility:

- **Practice**: Provide a structured environment but allow for flexibility when necessary.

- **Common-sense**: A balanced approach helps children feel secure but also allows for growth, creativity, and adaptability.

8. Creating a Safe Emotional Environment:

- **Practice**: Show love, affection, and reassurance regularly, especially during times of stress or uncertainty.

- **Common-sense**: A supportive emotional environment helps children feel safe, valued, and secure in their relationship with you.

9. Teaching Empathy:

- **Practice**: Teach your child to recognise and respect the feelings of others, and encourage compassionate behaviour.

- **Common-sense**: Teaching empathy fosters kindness and emotional intelligence, helping children develop healthy relationships with others.

10. Setting Realistic Expectations:

- **Practice**: Set developmentally appropriate goals for your child and be patient with their growth.

- **Common-sense**: Setting realistic expectations based on your child's age and ability ensures that they are not overwhelmed and can achieve success gradually.

11. Spending Quality Time Together:

- **Practice**: Engage in activities that strengthen your bond with your child, such as reading, playing, or talking.

- **Common-sense**: Quality time nurtures the parent-child relationship, creates lasting memories, and allows for open communication.

12. **Encouraging Healthy Habits:**

    - **Practice**: Promote healthy habits such as regular exercise, nutritious meals, and adequate sleep.

    - **Common-sense**: Healthy habits contribute to your child's physical and mental well-being, setting the foundation for lifelong health.

13. **Being Patient and Calm in Difficult Situations:**

    - **Practice**: Stay calm and patient when your child is acting out or upset, and use calming techniques to de-escalate situations.

    - **Common-sense**: Remaining calm teaches your child emotional regulation and prevents conflicts from escalating.

14. **Being Flexible with Mistakes:**

    - **Practice**: Allow your child to make mistakes and learn from them, providing guidance instead of harsh punishment.

    - **Common-sense**: Mistakes are learning opportunities, and allowing your child to experience them fosters resilience and problem-solving skills.

15. **Creating a Positive and Supportive Environment for Learning:**

    - **Practice**: Encourage a love for learning by being supportive, helping with homework, and praising efforts.

- **Common-sense**: A positive attitude toward education promotes curiosity, self-motivation, and a growth mindset in your child.

16. **Setting a Good Example for Healthy Relationships:**

    - **Practice**: Show your child how to build healthy, respectful relationships with others, including family members and friends.

    - **Common-sense**: Modelling healthy relationships teaches your child how to interact respectfully with others, building their social skills and emotional intelligence.

17. **Teaching Problem-Solving Skills:**

    - **Practice**: Guide your child through solving problems independently by encouraging them to think through different solutions.

    - **Common-sense**: Teaching problem-solving helps children build critical thinking skills and prepares them to handle challenges independently.

18. **Giving Space for Self-Expression:**

    - **Practice**: Allow your child to express their thoughts, feelings, and opinions, even if you disagree.

    - **Common-sense**: Encouraging self-expression promotes self-confidence, helps children understand their emotions, and strengthens their communication skills.

19. **Maintaining a Positive Home Environment:**

    - **Practice**: Foster a positive and nurturing environment at home, free of constant negativity or conflict.

- **Common-sense**: A positive environment helps your child feel safe, secure, and emotionally supported, creating a strong foundation for their overall well-being.

20. Teaching Responsibility for Actions:

- **Practice**: Hold your child accountable for their actions and teach them to take responsibility for their mistakes.

- **Common-sense**: Teaching accountability helps children develop a strong sense of responsibility and integrity as they grow.

These common-sense practices in parenting can help build a strong, supportive, and loving relationship between parents and children, fostering growth, emotional well-being, and respect within the family.

Examples of Common-Sense Practices in Professional Networks and Industry-Specific Associations

Being part of a professional network or industry-specific association can provide numerous benefits for career growth, collaboration, and knowledge sharing. Here are common-sense practices that can help individuals maximise their involvement and effectiveness within these networks and associations:

1. **Building Genuine Relationships:**

   - **Practice**: Engage with others in a sincere and authentic way, focusing on building real connections rather than just transactional interactions.

   - **Common-sense**: Genuine relationships foster trust and collaboration, which are essential for long-term success in professional networks.

2. **Actively Participating in Events and Activities:**

   - **Practice**: Attend meetings, webinars, conferences, and other events regularly to stay updated and build visibility within the association.

- **Common-sense**: Active participation allows you to stay informed about industry trends and helps establish your presence in the community.

3. Offering Help and Expertise:

- **Practice**: Share your knowledge, experience, or resources with others in your professional network whenever possible.

- **Common-sense**: By contributing to others' growth, you create goodwill and establish yourself as a valuable and helpful member of the community.

4. Networking with a Purpose:

- **Practice**: Approach networking with clear goals, such as learning new skills, finding potential partners, or expanding your influence in the industry.

- **Common-sense**: Purposeful networking helps you focus on building meaningful connections that align with your professional aspirations.

5. Staying Updated on Industry Trends:

- **Practice**: Regularly read industry publications, follow thought leaders, and stay informed about emerging trends and challenges in your field.

- **Common-sense**: Staying up-to-date enables you to bring relevant knowledge to the table and participate in informed discussions within your network.

6. Respecting Others' Time and Boundaries:

- **Practice**: Be mindful of others' time, especially when reaching out for advice, collaboration, or meetings. Be clear about the purpose of your communication.

- **Common-sense**: Respect for time and boundaries fosters positive interactions and helps maintain professional relationships.

7. Seeking Out Mentorship and Offering Guidance:

- **Practice**: Seek mentorship from experienced professionals while also offering guidance to those with less experience.

- **Common-sense**: A strong network thrives on reciprocal mentorship, where both learning and teaching take place to uplift the entire group.

8. Engaging in Collaborative Projects:

- **Practice**: Collaborate on projects, research, or community initiatives within your network or association to build trust and showcase your skills.

- **Common-sense**: Collaboration fosters innovation, provides opportunities for growth, and strengthens relationships within the network.

9. Being Transparent and Honest:

- **Practice**: Maintain transparency about your intentions, goals, and challenges when engaging with others in the network.

- **Common-sense**: Honesty builds credibility and trust, essential foundations for strong professional relationships.

10. Maintaining Regular Communication:

- **Practice**: Keep in touch with key members of your network through occasional check-ins, updates, or sharing useful resources.

- **Common-sense**: Regular communication keeps you on others' radars and ensures you remain a relevant and connected member of the network.

11. **Being Open to Constructive Feedback:**

- **Practice**: Be receptive to feedback and criticism from others within your network, viewing it as an opportunity for personal and professional growth.

- **Common-sense**: Embracing feedback fosters continuous improvement and shows others that you value their insights and contributions.

12. **Respecting Professional Etiquette:**

- **Practice**: Always follow industry-specific professional etiquette in your interactions, including using appropriate communication styles and respecting professional norms.

- **Common-sense**: Adhering to etiquette helps you maintain a positive reputation and ensures your interactions are professional and respectful.

13. **Contributing to Group Discussions and Forums:**

- **Practice**: Participate in group discussions, forums, and social media groups related to your industry by sharing knowledge and offering thoughtful comments.

- **Common-sense**: Actively engaging in discussions helps you stay visible and relevant within your professional community, showcasing your expertise.

14. Utilising the Association's Resources:

- **Practice**: Make the most of the resources provided by your professional association, such as training programmes, networking events, and industry reports.

- **Common-sense**: Leveraging available resources enhances your knowledge and capabilities, improving your value within the association.

15. Respecting Diversity and Inclusion:

- **Practice**: Embrace diversity and foster an inclusive environment by respecting different perspectives, cultures, and backgrounds within your network.

- **Common-sense**: Inclusion enhances collaboration and innovation, creating a more dynamic and forward-thinking professional environment.

16. Building a Personal Brand Within the Network:

- **Practice**: Work on developing and promoting your personal brand within the association through speaking opportunities, published content, or project involvement.

- **Common-sense**: A strong personal brand helps you stand out and attract more opportunities for collaboration, leadership, and career advancement.

17. Being Accountable and Reliable:

- **Practice**: Honour commitments and deliver on promises within your network, whether in collaborative projects or networking exchanges.

- **Common-sense**: Reliability builds trust and respect, ensuring that others view you as a dependable and valuable network member.

18. **Using Social Media Wisely:**

- **Practice**: Use social media to share industry insights, promote events, and connect with professionals in your field while maintaining a professional tone.

- **Common-sense**: Social media can be a powerful tool for growing your professional network, as long as it's used thoughtfully and professionally.

19. **Recognising and Celebrating Others' Achievements:**

- **Practice**: Acknowledge and celebrate the accomplishments of others in your professional network, whether through congratulations or public recognition.

- **Common-sense**: Celebrating others' successes creates goodwill, strengthens relationships, and encourages a positive and supportive network culture.

20. **Staying Accountable to Your Network:**

- **Practice**: Take responsibility for your role and contributions within the network, ensuring you fulfil your obligations and support others in the group.

- **Common-sense**: Accountability builds trust and ensures the network remains functional and productive for everyone involved.

These common-sense practices are crucial for creating and maintaining strong, meaningful relationships within professional networks and industry-specific associations. By applying these practices, you can expand your influence, learn from others, and contribute to the growth of your industry community.

Examples of Common-Sense as an Employee

1. **Punctuality and Time Management:**

   - **Common-sense**: Arriving on time and meeting deadlines shows respect for the workplace and helps maintain productivity. Being late can disrupt team schedules and project timelines.

2. **Clear Communication:**

   - **Common-sense**: Keeping colleagues and managers informed about the status of tasks, seeking clarification when needed, and addressing concerns promptly leads to smoother work relationships and efficient workflows.

3. **Taking Responsibility for Mistakes:**

   - **Common-sense**: Acknowledging errors and taking responsibility for them rather than blaming others demonstrates integrity and accountability, helping to build trust with your team and managers.

4. Respecting Work Boundaries:

- **Common-sense**: Understanding and respecting colleagues' personal space and work hours contributes to a positive and collaborative work environment.

5. Being Proactive and Taking Initiative:

- **Common-sense**: Anticipating needs and taking action without being asked, such as suggesting improvements or offering help, shows a willingness to contribute and demonstrates leadership potential.

6. Adapting to Change:

- **Common-sense**: Accepting and adjusting to new systems, processes, or responsibilities rather than resisting them helps ensure continued growth and adaptability in the workplace.

7. Maintaining Professionalism:

- **Common-sense**: Keeping interactions polite, respectful, and professional at all times, whether in person or online, creates a positive image and fosters a respectful work culture.

8. Being a Team Player:

- **Common-sense**: Collaborating well with others, sharing ideas, and supporting team efforts leads to better results and builds strong working relationships with colleagues.

9. Maintaining a Positive Attitude:

- **Common-sense**: Approaching challenges with a positive and solution-focused mindset can help you overcome obstacles and contribute to a more productive and harmonious work environment.

10. Taking Care of Your Health and Well-being:

- **Common-sense**: Managing your health and stress levels, such as taking regular breaks, staying hydrated, and balancing work-life commitments, ensures sustained productivity and prevents burnout.

These practices are fundamental to creating a productive, respectful, and harmonious work environment, while also advancing your career growth and fostering positive relationships with colleagues and managers.

Examples of Common-Sense as an Entrepreneur

1. Understanding Your Market:

- **Common-sense**: Conducting thorough market research before launching a product or service helps ensure there's demand, reducing the risk of failure. It's important to understand your customers' needs, preferences, and pain points.

2. Starting Small and Scaling Gradually:

- **Common-sense**: Rather than diving into massive investments, testing your business idea on a smaller scale first allows for valuable feedback and minimises financial risk. Scaling gradually enables sustainable growth.

3. Staying Focused on Your Core Business:

- **Common-sense**: While diversification can be appealing, it's crucial to stay focused on your core product or service that aligns with your strengths and market needs, rather than spreading yourself too thin.

4. Budgeting and Financial Management:

- **Common-sense**: Keeping a close eye on cash flow, managing expenses, and maintaining a healthy budget are fundamental for business sustainability. It's important to ensure the business is financially viable before taking on larger commitments.

5. Building Strong Relationships:

- **Common-sense**: Networking and building strong relationships with customers, suppliers, partners, and investors is key to long-term success. Trust and collaboration are the foundation of a successful business.

6. Being Adaptable to Change:

- **Common-sense**: The business landscape is constantly evolving. Being open to pivoting your business model or adopting new technologies when necessary ensures your business remains competitive and resilient.

7. Hiring the Right People:

- **Common-sense**: Hiring employees or partners who are not only skilled but also align with your company's vision and values helps ensure smooth operations and reduces friction within the team.

8. Setting Realistic Goals:

- **Common-sense**: Setting achievable and measurable goals, rather than overambitious or vague targets, helps maintain focus and motivates you and your team to work towards tangible results.

9. Seeking Mentorship and Advice:

- **Common-sense**: No entrepreneur knows everything. Seeking advice from mentors or industry experts can help you avoid common mistakes, gain new perspectives, and refine your strategies.

10. Staying Resilient in the Face of Failure:

- **Common-sense**: Failure is part of the entrepreneurial journey. Learning from mistakes, remaining resilient, and using setbacks as opportunities to grow and improve is essential for long-term success.

These common-sense practices help entrepreneurs navigate the complex world of business, make informed decisions, and build sustainable, thriving ventures.

Examples of Common-Sense in Leadership Roles

1. Leading by Example:

- **Common-sense**: As a leader, your actions speak louder than words. Demonstrating the behaviours, work ethic, and values you expect from your team sets a strong example and fosters respect and trust.

2. Clear and Transparent Communication:

- **Common-sense**: Open, honest communication is essential for effective leadership. Ensuring your team understands goals, expectations, and changes helps prevent confusion and misalignment, creating a positive work environment.

3. Empowering Your Team:

- **Common-sense**: Delegating authority and trusting your team to make decisions fosters empowerment and engagement. Micromanaging only stifles creativity and initiative, so it's important to let your team take ownership of their roles.

4. Providing Constructive Feedback:

- **Common-sense**: Giving regular and constructive feedback helps your team grow and improve. Acknowledging successes while offering guidance for improvement fosters a culture of continuous learning.

5. Being Approachable and Available:

- **Common-sense**: Leaders should make themselves accessible to their team members. Being approachable creates an environment where employees feel comfortable sharing ideas, concerns, and feedback.

6. Making Decisions Based on Facts, Not Emotions:

- **Common-sense**: Leaders must use logic and data when making decisions, not letting personal biases or emotions cloud their judgement. Thoughtful, evidence-based decisions lead to better outcomes and stronger leadership.

7. Fostering a Positive Work Culture:

- **Common-sense**: Creating an inclusive and supportive work environment is essential for team morale. Leaders should model respect, appreciation, and collaboration to ensure a healthy and productive workplace culture.

8. Adapting to Change:

- **Common-sense**: Leaders must remain flexible and adaptable in the face of change. Whether it's a market shift, technological advancements, or organisational changes, a successful leader embraces new challenges and guides the team through transitions.

9. Encouraging Work-Life Balance:

- **Common-sense**: Leaders should prioritise work-life balance, both for themselves and their team. Promoting a healthy balance ensures employees stay energised, productive, and motivated in the long run.

10. Recognising and Celebrating Achievements:

- **Common-sense**: Acknowledging the contributions and successes of your team boosts morale and motivates employees to continue performing at a high level. Celebrating both big and small wins reinforces a culture of appreciation.

These common-sense practices help leaders foster trust, inspire their teams, and navigate challenges with confidence, all while maintaining a focus on long-term success and organisational health.

Examples of Common-Sense in Business

1. **Customer Focus:**

   - **Common-sense**: Prioritise customer satisfaction by understanding their needs and delivering value. A business can only thrive if it consistently meets or exceeds customer expectations.

2. **Managing Cash Flow:**

   - **Common-sense**: Always keep an eye on cash flow. Ensuring that your business has enough liquidity to cover operating expenses and unexpected costs is essential for long-term sustainability.

3. **Adapting to Market Changes:**

   - **Common-sense**: The market is constantly evolving. Business leaders should be flexible and open to adjusting products, services, and strategies in response to shifts in demand, competition, and technology.

4. Effective Time Management:

- **Common-sense**: Time is one of the most valuable resources. Prioritising tasks, setting clear goals, and avoiding procrastination ensures that important activities are completed efficiently and effectively.

5. Building a Strong Team:

- **Common-sense**: Surround yourself with capable, motivated people who bring complementary skills to the table. A strong, cohesive team is one of the most critical factors for business success.

6. Monitoring Competitors:

- **Common-sense**: Keep track of competitors to stay informed about trends, pricing, and innovations. This helps you stay competitive and adjust your strategy if necessary to maintain an edge.

7. Simplifying Processes:

- **Common-sense**: Streamlining operations and eliminating unnecessary complexities saves time, reduces costs, and improves customer satisfaction. Efficiency should always be a priority in every business process.

8. Understanding Legal and Compliance Requirements:

- **Common-sense**: Comply with all relevant laws and regulations in your industry. Not adhering to legal and compliance standards can result in costly fines, damage to reputation, and business shutdowns.

9. **Focusing on Quality:**

- **Common-sense**: Delivering high-quality products and services should be non-negotiable. Quality drives customer loyalty, brand reputation, and long-term success.

10. **Seeking Feedback and Continuous Improvement:**

- **Common-sense**: Actively seek feedback from employees, customers, and business partners. Use this feedback to identify areas for improvement, innovate, and ensure the business stays relevant and competitive.

These common-sense practices in business help ensure smooth operations, customer satisfaction, and long-term growth. By applying these principles, businesses can build strong foundations and remain competitive in their respective industries.

Examples of Common-Sense Practices for Road Traffic

1. **Adhering to Speed Limits:**

   - **Common-sense**: Always drive within the posted speed limits. It ensures safety, reduces the risk of accidents, and helps maintain smooth traffic flow.

2. **Using Turn Signals:**

   - **Common-sense**: Always use your turn signals when changing lanes or making turns. This alerts other drivers to your intentions, reducing the chances of collisions and misunderstandings.

3. **Maintaining Safe Following Distance:**

   - **Common-sense**: Keep a safe distance between your vehicle and the one in front of you. This gives you time to react to sudden stops or changes in traffic conditions.

4. **Yielding to Pedestrians:**

   - **Common-sense**: Always stop for pedestrians at crosswalks. This not only protects lives but is required by traffic laws in most places.

5. Avoiding Distracted Driving:

- **Common-sense**: Avoid distractions such as texting, talking on the phone, or eating while driving. Staying focused on the road reduces the likelihood of accidents.

6. Following Traffic Lights and Signs:

- **Common-sense**: Obey traffic signals, stop signs, and other road signs. These rules are in place to regulate the flow of traffic and ensure safety.

7. Stopping for Emergency Vehicles:

- **Common-sense**: When you hear sirens or see emergency vehicles with flashing lights, pull over and stop. This allows them to pass quickly and safely.

8. Using Seat Belts:

- **Common-sense**: Always wear your seat belt and ensure all passengers do the same. It's a simple practice that significantly reduces the risk of injury in case of an accident.

9. Being Courteous to Other Drivers:

- **Common-sense**: Show patience and courtesy on the road. Let others merge, avoid aggressive driving, and give space to vehicles in need of a lane change.

10. Driving Defensively:

- **Common-sense**: Always be prepared for the unexpected actions of other drivers. Stay alert, anticipate potential hazards, and be ready to react appropriately to keep yourself and others safe.

These common-sense practices help ensure that road traffic runs smoothly, minimising the chances of accidents and promoting a safer driving environment for everyone.

Examples of Common-Sense Practices in Public Spaces

1. **Respecting Personal Space:**

   - **Common-sense**: Be mindful of people's personal space in public areas. Avoid standing too close to others and respect their boundaries, especially in crowded places like buses, trains, or queues.

2. **Queuing Properly:**

   - **Common-sense**: Always wait your turn in a queue. Jumping the line or cutting in front of others is inconsiderate and disrupts the order.

3. **Keeping Noise Levels in Check:**

   - **Common-sense**: Maintain a reasonable noise level in public spaces. Avoid loud conversations, music, or phone calls in quiet places like libraries, hospitals, or public transportation.

4. **Cleaning Up After Yourself:**

   - **Common-sense**: Always dispose of your trash properly. Whether it's in a park, public restroom, or on the street, cleaning up after yourself ensures that public spaces remain tidy and pleasant for everyone.

5. Yielding to Others in Shared Spaces:

- **Common-sense**: In places like escalators, walkways, or elevators, stand to the side to allow others to pass if they are in a hurry. This makes the space more accessible and reduces congestion.

6. Respecting Local Norms and Etiquette:

- **Common-sense**: Follow the cultural norms and social etiquette of the place you're in. Whether it's removing shoes before entering a home, respecting silence in a temple, or dressing modestly in certain places, understanding local customs shows respect.

7. Not Blocking Pathways:

- **Common-sense**: Avoid standing, sitting, or leaving personal belongings in places that block walkways or entrances, like in malls, subway stations, or crowded streets. This ensures easy movement and access for others.

8. Sharing Public Amenities:

- **Common-sense**: In public spaces like parks, beaches, or gyms, share amenities like benches, tables, and equipment. Don't monopolise resources for long periods, and be considerate of others who may be waiting.

9. Being Polite and Courteous:

- **Common-sense**: Simple gestures like saying "excuse me," "please," and "thank you" when interacting with others in public spaces help create a more respectful and friendly environment.

10. **Being Aware of Your Surroundings:**

- **Common-sense**: Stay alert and be mindful of your surroundings in public spaces. Avoid distractions like looking at your phone while walking in busy areas to prevent accidents or collisions with others.

These common-sense practices contribute to a more respectful, organised, and enjoyable experience for everyone in public spaces.

Examples of Common-Sense Practices for Teenagers

1. **Respecting Authority Figures:**

   - **Common-sense**: Respect teachers, parents, coaches, and other authority figures. Listening to their guidance helps maintain order and provides opportunities for personal growth.

2. **Managing Time Wisely:**

   - **Common-sense**: Balancing schoolwork, extracurricular activities, and relaxation is crucial. Prioritise your tasks, avoid procrastination, and ensure that you set aside time for study and personal activities.

3. **Staying Safe Online:**

   - **Common-sense**: Be mindful of your privacy and security while using the internet. Avoid sharing personal information, and always think before posting on social media.

4. **Avoiding Peer Pressure:**

   - **Common-sense**: Stand firm in your values and make choices that align with your beliefs, even if it means saying no to peer pressure. It's important to trust your instincts and not succumb to negative influences.

5. Good Communication with Parents:

- **Common-sense**: Maintain open and honest communication with your parents about your activities, friends, and challenges. This builds trust and ensures they can support you in making responsible decisions.

6. Being Responsible with Money:

- **Common-sense**: Manage your allowance or earnings wisely. Save a portion, avoid impulsive purchases, and understand the value of money, which will help you make informed decisions as you get older.

7. Staying Active and Healthy:

- **Common-sense**: Prioritise physical activity and maintain a balanced diet. Avoid excessive junk food, and remember that good physical health supports mental clarity and energy for everyday tasks.

8. Avoiding Harmful Substances:

- **Common-sense**: Make responsible decisions regarding alcohol, tobacco, and drugs. Understand the long-term consequences of using harmful substances and choose to protect your health and future.

9. Respecting Others' Boundaries:

- **Common-sense**: Recognise the importance of respecting personal boundaries in relationships, both online and offline. Respecting others' space, privacy, and feelings helps build positive friendships and avoids conflict.

10. **Being Accountable for Actions:**

- **Common-sense**: Take responsibility for your actions, whether positive or negative. If you make a mistake, own up to it and learn from it, rather than blaming others or making excuses.

These common-sense practices help teenagers navigate their path towards adulthood by fostering personal growth, building responsible habits, and promoting healthy, respectful relationships with others.

Examples of Common-sense practices for travellers

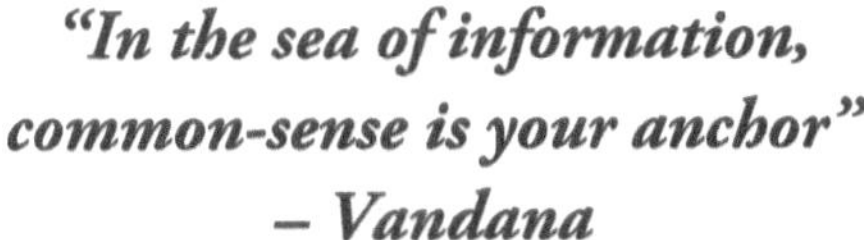

"In the sea of information,
common-sense is your anchor"
– Vandana

1. **Plan and Research Ahead:**

   - **Common-sense**: Before travelling, research your destination, local customs, weather conditions, and transport options. Being prepared helps avoid unnecessary surprises and ensures a smoother trip.

2. **Pack Smartly:**

   - **Common-sense**: Pack only what you need and keep your luggage organised. Include essential items like ID, tickets, medications, and chargers, and make sure to check the weather to pack appropriately.

3. **Keep Important Documents Safe:**

   - **Common-sense**: Always carry a copy of your passport, ID, tickets, and travel insurance information in case of loss or theft. Consider storing digital copies as a backup.

4. Follow Local Customs and Laws:

- **Common-sense**: Be respectful of the culture, customs, and laws of the country you're visiting. Familiarising yourself with local etiquette helps avoid misunderstandings and ensures a respectful visit.

5. Stay Aware of Your Surroundings:

- **Common-sense**: Stay alert in unfamiliar places, especially in crowded areas or when travelling at night. Avoid risky situations and trust your instincts for personal safety.

6. Use Reliable Transportation:

- **Common-sense**: When moving around, opt for safe, reliable modes of transportation like registered taxis, ride-sharing apps, or public transit. Avoid unmarked or suspicious vehicles.

7. Stay Hydrated and Eat Wisely:

- **Common-sense**: Drink plenty of water to stay hydrated, especially in hot climates, and eat foods that suit your dietary needs. Be cautious of street food if you're not accustomed to local hygiene standards.

8. Get Travel Insurance:

- **Common-sense**: Always have travel insurance that covers emergencies, medical expenses, and trip cancellations. It can save you from significant costs and stress in case of unexpected events.

9. Respect the Environment:

- **Common-sense**: Avoid littering, respect wildlife, and follow eco-friendly practices. Leave places as you found them to help preserve the environment for future travellers.

10. Have Emergency Contacts and Plans:

- **Common-sense**: Know emergency numbers and the location of the nearest embassy or consulate. Keep a list of emergency contacts and make sure family or friends know your travel plans.

By following these common-sense practices, travellers can ensure their safety, enjoyment, and respect for the places they visit while minimising potential risks.

Examples of Common-Sense Practices on Social Media

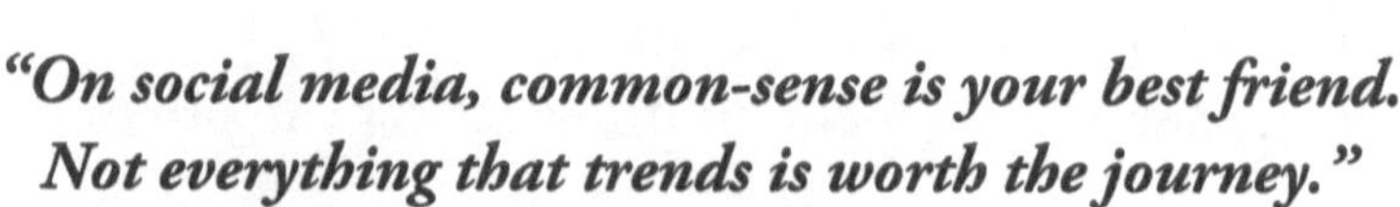

*"On social media, common-sense is your best friend.
Not everything that trends is worth the journey."*
– Vandana

1. **Think Before You Post:**

   - **Common-sense**: Always take a moment to consider the impact of your posts. Once something is online, it's hard to fully erase it, so make sure your content is respectful and appropriate.

2. **Maintain Privacy Settings:**

   - **Common-sense**: Adjust your privacy settings to control who can see your posts, personal information, and photos. Avoid oversharing, and be cautious about sharing sensitive details.

3. **Respect Others' Opinions:**

   - **Common-sense**: While it's great to engage in discussions, always respect differing opinions. Avoid heated arguments and instead foster healthy and respectful conversations.

4. Avoid Spreading Misinformation:

- **Common-sense**: Before sharing news or articles, verify the source and credibility of the content. Fact-check to avoid unintentionally spreading false information or rumours.

5. Use Appropriate Language:

- **Common-sense**: Always use respectful and professional language. Avoid offensive language, personal attacks, or inappropriate comments that could harm your online reputation.

6. Limit Excessive Posting:

- **Common-sense**: Don't overwhelm your followers with constant updates. Aim for a balance between engaging with your audience and avoiding spamming their feeds.

7. Be Cautious with Tags and Mentions:

- **Common-sense**: Only tag or mention people who are comfortable with being tagged. Ensure that your posts are relevant and respectful to others before tagging them in your content.

8. Protect Your Mental Health:

- **Common-sense**: Take breaks from social media if it's affecting your mood or mental well-being. Avoid comparing yourself to others and remember that social media often only shows a curated version of reality.

9. Use Strong Passwords and Two-Factor Authentication:

- **Common-sense**: Protect your accounts by using strong, unique passwords and enabling two-factor authentication. This helps safeguard your personal information from hackers.

10. **Be Mindful of Work-Life Balance:**

- **Common-sense**: Maintain a healthy balance between your personal and professional life on social media. Avoid sharing work-related frustrations publicly, and keep professional boundaries intact.

By following these common-sense practices, you can use social media responsibly, maintain your reputation, and engage in positive and meaningful interactions online.

The paradox of education is precisely this - that as one begins to become conscious, one begins to examine the society in which he is being educated.
– James Baldwin

How will you navigate the common-sense paradox, using it as a catalyst for personal and collective evolution?